Austin's Three Forms of Government

Austin's Three Forms of Government

by Stuart A. MacCorkle

The Naylor Company
Book Publishers of the Southwest
San Antonio, Texas

Library of Congress Cataloging in Publication Data

MacCorkle, Stuart Alexander, 1903-
   Austin's three forms of government.

   Includes bibliographical references.
   1. Austin, Tex.—Politics and government.
I. Title.
JS567.2.A2M3   320.4'764'31   73-1954
ISBN 0-8111-0476-1

Contents

Preface

THE POWER STRUCTURE OF MOST COMMUNI-
ties grinds out mayors and councilmen without too much
direct control by the voters. The insiders tend to exercise
control over most phases of municipal government. At least,
this is the case until a crisis arises, at which time the wrath
of the public is aroused and both the machinery and the
personnel of government are changed in one fell swoop. This
has been, by and large, the history of Austin's city government. There seems to exist in the heart of man an impetus
of optimism which, even in the dark days, he keeps dreaming
about brighter days to come.

This is good.

A history of Austin city government has never been
written. This is not an attempt to do so. Austin has operated
under the three major forms of city government. Here an
effort is made to analyze each form in terms of efficiency
in administration, controls exercised — both internal and
external and by whom, and the services provided the
citizens.

The author has been a resident of Austin since the early
thirties and has not only been an observer of the local
scene, but an active participant in her community and
governmental activities.

The first period, mayor-aldermanic government, 1840-
1909, is most difficult, if not impossible to treat in an
objective and meaningful manner — the materials necessary

to make such feasible are not available. The second period, commission government, 1909-1926, one finds much easier; the records for the most part are good, but those who participated in the activities of the time have passed from the stage. The last period, extending from the adoption of council-manager in 1926 to present is charged with perplexities because the author is too familiar with the problems and the personalities involved. Being fair and objective under such conditions is hard.

But after all the purpose of this little book is to give the writer's impressions of Austin's city government past and present. Specifically, I have expressed some thoughts on how the government of this city has operated, how it might be fashioned in order that the people to whom it belongs might be better served.

The polite thing to do would be to record the names of the many officials, civic leaders, and citizens with whom I have consulted and talked during the preparation of this manuscript. To do so would be impossible.

I do want to acknowledge my deep appreciation to Walter E. Long for his assistance and encouragement in this undertaking. Also I shall always remember with warmth and gratitude Mrs. Elsie Woosley, City Clerk and Mrs. Grace Monroe, Associate City Clerk, the personnel at the Austin-Travis County Collection, and the many city officials and employees at city hall who not only graciously provided my many requests for information, but who did so much to make my years at the municipal building in Austin some of the most fruitful of my life.

To Guiton Morgan and the late Walter E. Seaholm who introduced me to my first sojourn into active municipal administration, I owe much. They served as city managers during my first stint as a member of the Austin city council. Upon my return to the council years later, Managers Robert E. Tinstman and Lynn H. Andrews gave me a refresher course in municipal administration and exposed me to much that is learned in no other way than by hard knocks.

Andrews not only believed in, and talked about efficient management — he lived and practiced it.

I cannot close without expressing my appreciation and thanks to Mrs. Deborah G. Barlow, a graduate student in history at The University of Texas, Austin, working under Dr. Robert C. Cotner of that department who did much of the research on Chapter III. Her careful work and enthusiasm for the subject matter made a sometimes dry topic live.

Special acknowledgment is made to Mrs. Ruth Landress for her excellent work in preparing and typing the final manuscript.

Stuart A. MacCorkle

I

Introduction

AUSTIN — THE CENTER OF TEXAS GOVERN-
ment and the seat of The University of Texas — is the fastest-
growing state capital in the United States. It is located on
the Colorado River about midway between the Lower Rio
Grande Valley on the south and the Red River on the north.
To its west is the Hill Country with vast ranching areas and
on the southwest and east are the rich farming regions of the
central blacklands.

The story of Austin, Texas has been — they come, they
see, they stay — for over a century now. This, a rapidly
growing city with a relatively mild climate, a cultural
atmosphere, and recreational facilities of the nearby hills
and lakes, all make it a charming place to live.

The population of Austin has, from the earliest days,
been quite homogenous in character. Settlers, largely of
British extraction, came to Texas from all of the other
southern states. According to the Census of Population of

1

1970, the figure stood at 251,808, a population jump of more than fifty percent during the last decade. This population is largely of Anglo-American descent, with approximately fourteen percent Mexican-American and twelve percent black. The citizenship of Austin includes government officials, university and college professors and administrative staffs, businessmen, lawyers, doctors and dentists, professional and semiprofessional persons far more numerous than are found in most cities of similar size. The five colleges and universities located in the city had a total enrollment of approximately 42,500 students for the fall semester of 1971.

Austin is also the seat of Travis County. The city's population comprises the bulk of the county's population of approximately 300,000. Numbered in this figure are the inhabitants of the five general law cities of Pflugerville, Rollingwood, Sunset Valley, West Lake Hills, and San Leandro, with a combined population of about 2,827. Each of these cities is located just on the outskirts of Austin. A few miles from Austin and within Travis County are the general law cities of Elgin, Manor, and Round Rock. The largest of these is Elgin with a population of around 4,000. The Capital Area Planning Council, which was organized in June of 1970, is also headquartered in Austin. The Council is composed of Bastrop, Blanco, Burnet, Caldwell, Fayette, Hays, Lee, Llano, Travis, and Williamson counties.

The Austin Independent School District is, by and large, coterminous with the City of Austin which levies and collects the taxes for the schools and provides for the issuance of school bonds. As of this writing the city has a tax rate of $1.29 per $100 assessed evaluation and the Austin Independent School District a rate of $1.60 per $100 assessed evaluation. To present, few taxpayers have dared to raise questions regarding the expenditure of school funds. They have not been so restrained with respect to city activities. Approximately fifty percent of the real property within the City of Austin is tax exempt.

2

Early History

Austin was founded as the Capital City of The Republic of Texas, as the City of Washington was built to be our Nation's Capital. On the fifteenth day of January, 1839, under the administration of President Lamar, the Congress of the Republic passed an act creating a Commission of five members whose duty it was to find a permanent location for the capital. The Commission visited a number of places but finally recommended that the capital be located at a spot on the Colorado River known as Waterloo, which is the site of present-day Austin. "The higher elevation and Freedom from Fevers of the Coast country" were listed, among others, as reasons for the selection of this location.

Under the act, A. C. Horton, J. W. Burton, William Menifee, Isaac Campbell and Louis P. Cooke were selected as commissioners. The act also provided "that the name of the site shall be the City of Austin." The city was thus named in honor of Stephen F. Austin, early pioneer, and Father of Texas.

It is said that Waterloo, the selected site, consisted of only a few families, and that the rival town of Montopolis, about three miles below it, could boast of less. While it is reported that the latter insisted very strongly on being chosen as the capital, and that quite a bit of jealousy grew up between the two, most of these differences vanished at the first Indian Raid.

The beauty of the scenery, the central location, and the purity of the atmosphere apparently dominated the actions of those who chose Waterloo as the site for the new capital and not a desire on their part for personal gain or the enlargement of their own purses or those of their friends. A community of only a few families in the late 1830s, by 1840 grew up overnight into a town dotted with frame houses and log cabins, devoid of any semblance of order or civic display. Streets and sidewalks were practically unheard of and walking about town in rainy weather was out of the question.

The population in 1840 was in the neighborhood of 856 persons, most of whom were white, grown males.

Late in 1839, the *Austin City Gazette* was established and shortly afterwards, another paper came into being which was known as the *Sentinel.* They were both weekly newspapers.

The Fourth Texas Congress, on December 27, 1839, passed an act providing for incorporating the City of Austin. At this time, Austin was in Bastrop County, as Travis County had not been organized. On January 13, 1840, an election under the charter was held for city officers which resulted in the election of Judge Edwin N. Waller as the first Mayor of Austin. The duties of the office at that time were not very onerous — the principal one being that of policing the town.

Prior to becoming Mayor, Edwin N. Waller had distinguished himself as one of the four delegates from Brazoria County to the Convention of 1836 at Washington-on-the-Brazos and a signer of the Declaration of Independence. As one of the committee which framed the constitution of the Texas Republic, his name is fourth on the list of its signers. Waller had also been appointed to survey the land for the new capital and to sell lots and to construct public buildings in Austin preceding the moving of the seat of government from Houston.

However, Mayor Waller resigned from his office before his term expired and moved to a farm in Austin County, later named Waller County.

Economic Life

Income is the lifeblood of any economy. Austin's income has been relatively high when compared with other areas of the state. It should be noted also that this income has not experienced wide fluctuations which are common to heavily industrialized cities. Business failures have been relatively few for a number of decades and the per capita expenditure for goods at retail stores and for business and personal services has exceeded the average for the state and for most cities of comparable size. At the same time, one does not find large industrial sections, huge factories, oil fields, refineries, or other evidences of sources of income common to many metropolitan areas. As a matter of fact, not until two or three decades ago have industries been encouraged in Austin.

An abundance of water is perhaps Austin's greatest natural resource. The taming of the Colorado River has stimulated confidence in the development of the area and has assured Austin of an adequate water supply for continued growth and industrial development. There are few cities in the whole Southwest area so fortunate.

The growth of Austin has been associated closely with the expansion in activities of the federal, state, and local governments and in the increased enrollment at The University of Texas at Austin. Agriculture, manufacturing, and trading also have contributed to the city's economic growth.

However, education and government have in the past dominated the economic life of the city, just as the tower of the Library and Administration Building at the university and the dome of the capitol have dominated the skyline. In some respects this is past tense today, for we have appearing on the Austin skyline a number of highrise apartments, banks and office buildings.

There was a period when industries were not encouraged to locate or expand in Austin. This attitude too has been altered within recent years. The advent of technology has led to the mushrooming of a number of scientific-based firms in or on the outskirts of the city. Some of these are the I.B.M. Corporation, Texas Instruments, Glastron Boat Company, Westinghouse Electric Corporation, Jefferson Chemical Company, Nalle Plastics, Inc., Holloway Dynamics Company, Tracor, Inc., Adams Extract Company, Economy Furniture Company, Woodward, Inc., Steck Company, Publishers, and U.S. Steel Homes to name a few of Austin's major industries. Industries such as these appeal to employees in all levels of education, skills, technology, and salary. Austin's total labor force as of late 1971 was approximately 142,000 persons.

The military activities in the Austin area are considerable. The Bergstrom Air Force Base, about ten miles southeast of the city, is a permanent installation with 3,000 acres and a personnel of 5,700. It is headquarters of the 12th Air Force. Austin, also, is the site of one of four national quarters for the Air Force Reserve. In addition, Camp Mabry, located in West Austin, is a permanent National Guard Center.

Austin is situated central to the entire southern half of the nation, and centered in a rapidly growing state and southwestern market, with good air, rail, and interstate highway radials to all points. Centered among Texas' three largest cities — Dallas, Houston, and San Antonio — and less than two hundred miles from each, without, at the moment, too many herculean metropolitan problems. Within its boundaries there are over 284 churches, three colleges, two universities, two theological seminaries, over 244 headquarters of state and national associations and organizations, twelve banks, thirty-seven insurance companies, four television stations, and seven hospitals.

Austin combines an academic environment, a rich historical and cultural heritage with a mild climate, fresh air and water, and year-round outdoor recreation opportunities.

The famed Barton Springs natural pool's daily flow of sixty-eight-degree crystal clear water the year around has no equal anywhere in the land. When one thinks of Austin, he thinks of Barton Springs.

II

What Makes for Good City Government

ON THREE OCCASIONS, THE CITIZENS OF Austin have selected a form of government to provide municipal services. The first two were replaced and today there has been talk of moving in retrograde, and replace the present council-manager government with one of the earlier forms.

Perhaps the form of government is not so important as the citizen activity it engenders, which is the key to the successful community.

Only one of the three forms of government under which Austin has been operated is dependent upon professional management; the others are politically inspired, politically operated, and politically controlled. Indeed, council-manager government may be subverted by the politicians, as we shall see.

Simply, manager government is designed to remove the day-to-day operations of the municipality from the political arena, in an effort to obtain businesslike operations that provide the best and most service with the least tax burden. The choice is between decisions by professional politicians or professional administrators.

Municipal government has grown more complex than police and fire protection, an occasional street paving, and picking up garbage. Even the mundane and necessary activities have grown enormously, as well as hundreds of other areas of community service. As services have expanded, so have the costs, and city government has become a major financial enterprise in any community.

What calibre of individual or group of individuals do we want to plan, build, finance and administer these services? Professional politicians or professional administrators?

If contracts are to be awarded, do we want the best and lowest bid, or do we give the contract to "good ole Joe," who needs the money because he is the friend of some city official? Professional politician or professional administrator?

And so it might go on.

The citizens get the kind of government they want, or as a cynic once said, "what they deserve."

Mr. Charles Abrams, writing in *The New York Times* Book Review on December 15, 1965, thus defined a city:

> A city, even an American city, is a pulsating product of the human hand and mind, reflecting man's history, his struggle for freedom, his creativity, his genius — and his selfishness and errors. It is the tablet on which man's story is written, the record of those who built a skyscraper or a picture window, fought a pitched battle for a play street, created a bookshop or bakeshop that mattered. It is a composite of trials and defeats, of settlement houses, churches, and schoolhouses, of aspirations, images, and memories. A city has values as well as slums, excitement as well as conflict; it has a personality that has not yet been obliterated by its highways

and gas stations; it has a spirit as well as a set of arteries and a voice that speaks the hopes as well as the disappointments of its people.

The Citizen

Every city may become a great city and well has it been said, "Cities are what men make them." James Bryce in his monumental commentary on *The American Commonwealth* asserted that the "ordinary American voter does not object to mediocrity in his candidates for public office." This was Bryce's view of nineteenth century conditions. In the twentieth century there seems to be a very great danger the American might simply not object, period. One is reminded of the adage that we are a people capable of achieving the highest calibre of government which we demand, but of getting the lowest brand which we are willing to endure.

How do you fight city hall? It is not easy. You do it by urging your professional association or your union or trade association to become active. You do it by individual effort, by making a pest of yourself at city hall or collecting names to petitions. You may do it by joining a citizen group which hires a paid lobbyist to counteract the influence of the corporate lobby. A good example is the Sierra Club, which has done this in the environmental field. If there is no group which suits your interest, then maybe you should organize one.

It is being more and more realized today that good government is not achieved only on election day, but through constant, day-to-day effort on our part and on the part of our neighbors. We are increasingly aware that our vote, important as it is, is not really effective unless it is backed up by an active, continuing interest in what happens as a result of that vote.

Government is everybody's business. What is required by everyone, actually, is good, active citizenship. The word *active* is the key to what we are seeking. It is passive citizenship just to live and to stay out of jail. It is only one step removed to vote just once in a while — to cast an occasional ballot and let it go at that.

To have a good city means an all-year job every year for more and more people. Being a good citizen or holding a public office is not a part-time job.

The Form of Government

We have attempted to emphasize the point that an organized citizenry is the most powerful voice heard in a democratic society. However, there is nothing automatic in the democratic process. It must have machinery through which to work. A form of government, therefore, is a piece of machinery. The citizen is the operator of the governmental machine. If he does not perform his job well, then no machinery will adequately function. On the other hand, it is admitted that one piece of machinery may be better than another piece in making the citizen's job easier.

Efficient, honest, and economic governmental operations are essential to the growth and well-being of any community. But there are few today who would agree in toto with Pope's oft-quoted couplet:

> For forms of government let fools contest;
> Whate'er is best administer'd is best.

Most of us desire good government, and most of us realize that there is a relationship between form of government and efficient administration. A good form of government will tend to encourage participation by the voters, attract more capable men into public service, and it will also facilitate their work after they have taken office. It is to be noted, however, that the form of government is only one factor in obtaining good government, but it is an important factor.

The machinery of government is not composed of laws

alone, or of men alone, but of both. The two are interdependent.

At the risk of fatiguing our reader, let us quote from Plato's *The Republic* written in 327 B.C. which has an ironic contemporary ring.

> All forms of government destroy themselves by carrying their basic principles to excess. The first form is monarchy, whose principle is unity of rule. Carried to excess, the rule is too unified. A monarchy takes too much power. The aristocracy rebel and establish an aristocracy whose main principle is that selected families rule. Carried to excess, somewhat large numbers of able men are left out, the middle classes join them in rebellion, and they establish a democracy whose principle is liberty. That principle, too, is carried to excess in the course of time. The democracies become too free, in politics and economics, in morals, even in literature and art, until at last even the puppy dogs in our home rise on their hind legs and demand their rights. . . . Disorder grows to such a point that a society will abandon all its liberty to anyone who can restore order.

But who reads Plato anymore?

The writer cannot help recalling the often-quoted phrase, "Governments, like clocks, go from the motion men give them; and as governments are made and moved by men, so they are ruined too."

No form of government will guarantee good government to a community. The resources of the city, the calibre of the elected officials, the quality of the city employees are all important factors. Intelligent citizen interest and participation, and the spirit of the community are all vital to the success of any plan.

Comparing and evaluating the forms of city government is a difficult task. In doing so, one must deal with such variables as personnel, functions and services, period of time,

11

methods of record keeping, and the ever-changing value of the American dollar. Any conclusions reached are necessarily approximate. In government the materials and exact conditions under which an experiment is tried at any given time can never be reproduced for some later experiment.

Austin's Governments

Much over a century of state government and almost one hundred years of university life within the city have contributed to the growth, character, and economic strength of Austin, the city with the Violet Crown. However, neither of these institutions has dominated Austin's city government. Town, gown, and capitol, by and large, have been independent of the other; at the same time there has prevailed a rather harmonious working relationship between the three over the years. The Austin Chamber of Commerce reflects this solidarity as it includes in its membership business, educational, and professional representatives.

Austin has lived under three forms of city government. The state charter granted in 1840 provided for mayor-council or mayor-aldermanic government. In 1909 the charter was amended to provide for a commission form of government. Finally, in 1924, under the home rule provision of the Texas constitution, the charter was again amended and the council-manager plan was adopted, but it did not go into effect until two years later, after much litigation. The latter form is in existence today.

Each form of government has been attacked by the groups not controlling it, but since the establishment of council-manager government, no group of any great strength has been disposed to demand a change in Austin's fundamental government structure.

III

Mayor-Aldermanic Government (1840-1909)

A STUDY OF AUSTIN CITY GOVERNMENT OF this period has never been made. Such an undertaking is beset with many difficulties, foremost of which is the lack of accurate official records. Council minutes for the period preceding November 1862 do not exist — they probably disappeared during the Civil War.

Again, these minutes until after 1900 were written in longhand and this does not lend to their easy deciphering. In some cases they are illegible. In the early years the city clerk was not always a meticulous keeper of the journal. Too often only brief summaries of council sessions are provided and in some instances the minutes are incomplete. Newspapers, city directories, diaries, and personal letters of individuals during the period often give sidelights and tell some interesting stories, but they do not reveal the day-to-day happenings at city hall.

Mayor and Aldermen

Election and Term

Old colonial traditions in city government had little effect upon Austin's governmental organization. The features to charter her course for the next forty or fifty years in municipal government were: elective mayor and aldermen, elective administrative officials, short terms of office, extension of suffrage, extension of the spoils system, and the genesis of a system of checks and balances.

Austin, as we have seen, was incorporated in 1840 when a state-granted charter provided for the mayor-aldermanic form of government. This charter was in keeping with the time, for apparently from 1840 to 1846 the mayor and eight aldermen were elected for a term of one year. In 1846 the number of aldermen was reduced to six, but the term of office remained the same. However, in 1857 the number was again increased to eight and it is very probable they were elected by wards, although we have little evidence to substantiate the use of a ward system until 1863. As of this date an alderman was elected from each of the eight wards. Ten years later this number was increased by the adding of wards nine and ten. It was believed that by so doing the expanding city would be better served.

With the election of November 8, 1883, a new system was inaugurated in accordance with a charter amendment of the previous April. The change provided that two men would be chosen by the voters of each ward to serve a term of two years. However, their terms were to be staggered. Therefore, upon their election in November 1883, the newly elected council members drew lots among themselves to determine who would serve a short term of one year. The remaining ten members were to serve the regular term of two years. This meant that each year an election would be held to fill the positions of the expired terms of ten

14

members. An election for the office of mayor was to be held only on alternating years.

The aldermen had the power to determine the boundary lines of the wards. However, the city charter of 1891 was amended to stipulate that there would be not more than eleven wards.[1] In June 1891, the board of aldermen added the eleventh ward and, correspondingly, called an election to provide for aldermen.[2] This brought the total membership to twenty-two, excluding the mayor.

Twenty-two was the maximum number of aldermen to serve the city from 1840 to 1909. However, a charter amendment in 1901 provided for a fourteen-man board, two members to be elected from each of seven wards. The terms of office of both the mayor and aldermen were designated as two years. This amended charter also stipulated that one alderman from each ward would be elected at large, while the other member would be elected from the voters of the ward.[3] This method first went into operation with the election of April 1903.

The board of aldermen supervised the conduction of all city elections. The dates of elections, their judges, and the polling places were all questions decided by this body. These powers, in combination with the power to canvass the election returns, gave the mayor and the board an opportunity to wield a strong hand over the election process. However, there is little recorded evidence of unethical conduct, with the exception of the claims against the election judges' electioneering tactics in 1895.[4] But a lack of recorded evidence is hardly sufficient reason to assume malpractice did not exist from time to time.

In the event of a contested election, the board of alder-

---

1 Texas, Congress, House, An *Act to Incorporate the City of Austin, to Grant It a New Charter and to Extend Its Boundaries,* H.B. 636, Sec. 3, 1891.

2 Austin City Council, *Minute Book H,* June 1, 1891, P. 140.

3 *Texas, House Bill,* 636, Sec. 5.

4 *Austin Statesman,* Dec. 16, 1895.

men made the final judgment upon the matter. An individual objecting to a particular election had the right to appear before the board and express his complaint. The winning candidate was also allowed to present a defense in his behalf. After hearing both sides, the board could declare the winner a legitimate one or call another election.[5]

Reconstruction Period

Brief mention should be made here of Austin's government during the Reconstruction Period. The entire municipal framework of government was altered during this time. The mayor and aldermen held their positions by virtue of gubernatorial appointment. As early as 1865, Gov. A. T. Hamilton appointed the mayor and filled a number of vacancies on the board left vacant by resignations. The amount of power wielded by the governor in city affairs is not easily ascertainable, but it seems reasonable to assume it was substantial. Members of the board were responsible to him by oath, and again he held the power of their appointment and removal.

Qualifications

Various city charters contained a limited number of qualifications for those holding the offices of mayor and aldermen. The most common of these were of a residential nature. For example, the 1878 charter required that they be citizens of the state and residents of Austin six months prior to the election. In addition, a candidate must have been a resident of the ward for at least thirty days preceding his election.[6] However, the 1891 charter contained a more flexible residence requirement — it merely demanded that

5 H.B. 636, Sec. 9.

6 Robertson, J. W., ed., *Charter and Revised Ordinances of the City of Austin*, (Austin: Texas Capitol Book and Job Office, 1878), Charter Art. 4, P. 9.

the candidate be a resident of the ward in which he ran for office.[7]

Frequently, city charters of the period added other restrictions to those seeking the offices of mayor and aldermen. The 1886 charter, as well as the one of 1891, prohibited members of the governing body from holding another city post at the same time. Charter sections also restricted the city official's power to use his position for personal gain. Neither the mayor nor the aldermen were permitted to be directly or indirectly involved in any contract or agreement in which the city was to pay or participate.[8]

The board of aldermen had the power to establish other requirements for the office, but no such ordinance or resolutions were found to have been passed concerning this matter.

If an alderman moved out of his ward he automatically vacated his position. The most frequent cause for vacancies on the board was this requirement of residency. Often aldermen moved from one area of the city to another or out of the city entirely. Other reasons for vacancies included ill health, business concerns, and death. The aldermen, by charter, could remove one of their own members by a two-thirds vote.[9] The impeachment process was not found to have been used between the years of 1840 and 1909.

Salaries and Meetings

Austin's policy makers have never been well paid. During the 1870s they received a remuneration of four dollars each per regular meeting and two dollars per special session, provided they attended in each case. During the mid-1880s they served without pay, but the 1891 charter provided for a payment of five dollars each per session, not to exceed ten dollars per month.[10]

---

7 Texas, H.B. 636, Sec. 4.
8 Robertson, op. cit., Art. 26, P. 28.
9 Ibid., Art. 27, P. 28.
10 Texas, H.B. 636, Sec. 16.

The mayor received a little more compensation for his services than did the aldermen for theirs. Salaries for both the mayor and aldermen frequently were set by city charter or ordinances or both, and their remuneration fluctuated from time to time. For instance, the mayor was paid $500 per annum in 1871[11] but by 1877 it jumped $200 per year.[12] In 1886 he received $600 per year[13] and for most of the nineties it remained around this figure.[14] Ordinarily the board of aldermen met once a week after 1865. Special sessions of the body might be called by the mayor or at the request of four or five aldermen.

Attendance at Meetings

Attendance at the board meetings was highly irregular. It was seldom that all members were present. As a matter of fact, some charters provided that a member could be fined for nonattendance and it was not too unusual for a charter provision to permit an absentee member to be charged one dollar for each session he missed.[15] It was the duty of the city marshal to attend all sessions for the purpose of rounding up the truant members, which he often did.

The mayor, too, was often guilty of absenteeism in those early years of Austin's city government. When this occurred, the president of the board replaced him as the presiding officer. It was customary for the board to elect a president from among their number, usually at the time of their installation. In the event that both the mayor and the president of the board of aldermen were absent, the group could elect a member to preside for the session. Regardless

---

11 *Minute Book* A, Feb. 13, 1871.

12 Robertson, op. cit., Art. 490, P. 141.

13 Ruggles, Gardner and Johnson, I.D., *Charter and Revised Civil and Criminal Ordinances*, Charter, Art. VIII, P. 18.

14 *American Statesman*, Dec. 16, 1895.

15 *Minute Book* E, Nov. 13, 1882.

of who chaired the session, he was entitled to execute the prerogatives of the mayor.

Composition

From 1840 to 1909, Austin's board of aldermen was predominantly white and masculine. No woman ever served on the city's policy-making body until 1948. The only Negroes to serve during this period were appointed by Governor Davis in February of 1871 and they served only until the first general election in November 1872.[16] The records do not indicate which two of the members were Negroes.[17]

Aldermen in Austin apparently did not come from any particular group or class within society. An examination of the professions and occupations of board members, as found in the city directories for the seventies, eighties, and nineties, reveals a great diversity of occupations. In this list one finds architects, contractors, builders, grocers, bookkeepers, gunsmiths, retailers of sporting goods, bricklayers, carpenters, liverymen, operators of freight lines, real estate and livestock dealers, brokers, jewelers, pawnbrokers, druggists, bar owners, owners of land and livestock companies, clerks in dry goods stores, owners of lumber companies, one dentist, one schoolteacher, and a few lawyers, but no doctors.

Powers

The board of aldermen had a wide variety of powers. Municipal powers not specifically assigned to other agencies were generally considered to be vested in the governing body. This body was first a local legislative body. Most of its time was spent in considering and passing ordinances for

---

[16] Barkley, Mary Star, *History of Austin and Travis County 1839-1899,* P. 108, Steck Co., Austin, 1963.
[17] Records do indicate the Negro members.

the government and welfare of the city. It also oversaw the administration of city affairs.

As an example, the 1891 Austin charter provided a general description of the board's function and powers: "That the city council shall have the care, management, and control of the city and its property and finances, except as may be herein otherwise specially provided for; and shall have the power to enact and ordain any and all ordinances not repugnant to the constitution and laws of the state, and such ordinances to alter, modify or repeal."[18]

During the early periods of Austin's city government no specialized departments existed; therefore the board of aldermen had all of the responsibility for every municipal service, including streets, water and sewer construction, citizen protection, health care, and the like. The 1878 charter includes a detailed list of these powers. For example, these included: right to levy taxes and issue bonds; regulation of night patrols; constructing city buildings; licensing and taxing merchants, retailers, grocers, and hotels; regulating bawdy houses and gambling places; preventing fires; regulating fences; inspecting food; determining bread weight and quality; setting standards of weights and measures; preventing the spread of illness; and the preventing of disorderly assemblages.[19] This catalogue is far from complete, but it illustrates the vast scope of the city's operation even at that date.

Method of Operation

In the discharge of its duties, the board functioned with a system of standing committees. The mayor determined the committees necessary and appointed the membership from among the aldermen. Usually two or three members composed a committee and each usually served on several

---

18 Texas, H.B. 636, Sec. 34.
19 Robertson, op. cit., Art. 6, pp. 11-13.

committees at a given time.[20] The business of the city government was handled through these standing committees. The committee made the necessary investigation of the matter assigned to it and reported to the body. This report usually took the form of recommendations for action to be taken on a specific issue. For example, the ordinance committee made recommendations for new ones or for changes in existing ordinances and drew the necessary drafts for the board's approval.

The number of standing committees varied from administration to administration, but the trend was toward increasing their numbers. By 1909, in addition to finance, cemetery, streets and market house, the following committees had been added: water and light, parks, fire, police, ordinances, claims and accounts, printing, sanitation and sewage, hospital, charity, purchasing, and city hall.[21]

Most of the vital decisions on legislative matters were made by these standing committees before the subject reached council floor. The board of aldermen was usually disposed to follow committee recommendations, though not bound to do so. One gets the impression that the board as a body seldom got the chance to express its views — it rubber-stamped committee reports.

Mayor

During the latter half of the nineteenth century the mayor was a rather influential person in Austin. He supervised municipal administration, though in many cases he did not control it. He played an important part in shaping legislation, and his powers of appointment were rather broad. More than any other person he represented all the

20 *Minute Book* A, Feb. 13, 1871, P. 45.
21 *Standing Committees of the City Council for the Term Ending April 1909*, Austin-Travis County Collection.

people of the city. Unlike the members of the board of aldermen, his viewpoint and his interests extended beyond the boundaries of a single ward. Being the official head of the city government he was expected to give a part of his time to social duties. By and large, many people had an exaggerated idea of the mayor's powers and influence. To many he was the "Father of all," able to ease every sorrow and right every wrong.

The powers of mayor during this period might be classified under three main heads: legislative, administrative, and judicial. Although he was the city's chief executive and was charged primarily with the enforcement of the laws, he also played a part in the shaping of legislation. Various charters directed him to make recommendations to the board of aldermen — "For the protection and improvement of the city's government and finances." He was required to issue detail reports on the condition of the city's finances. Usually these were scattered throughout the year, but the most important ones were those made upon his installation and the expiration of his term. Mayor T. B. Wheeler, upon his installation as the first elected mayor after Reconstruction, spoke in part as follows:

> In seeking to fulfill the functions of the office of mayor, my actions will be without reference to race, color, or nationality, unbiased by love and uninfluenced by prejudice.[22]

The outgoing gubernatorial appointee, John Glenn, on the same occasion had this comment:

> The benefits which Austin may have derived from our administration I attribute more to you [the council members] than to myself. You have restrained me in instances, doubtless where I was inclined to be too hasty,

---

22 *Minute Book* A, Nov. 16, 1872, P. 286.

and have spurred me up in others, where I may have been too tardy.[23]

The mayor apparently had no vote except in case of a tie; he did possess the power by virtue of being the presiding officer of the board to direct discussion in such a way that legislation was directly or indirectly effected as he might desire. In addition, Austin's mayors had the veto power, which they appear to have used rather sparingly. The occasions when his veto was overridden were rare, if ever. It required a two-thirds vote of the aldermen to override the mayor's veto.

Throughout the existence of mayor-aldermanic government in Austin, it may be said that the mayor was a dominant force at city hall. He was the chief administrative officer of the city. Serving with him and working more or less under his direction was the city's administrative staff. A need for some full-time administrative officers was recognized as early as 1840, when Austin had a recorder or clerk, a treasurer, and a city marshal. As the city grew and as the demands increased on the board of aldermen, additional offices were created by both charters and ordinances. In addition to those mentioned above there appeared a few years later the city attorney, assessor and collector of taxes, city engineer, city physician, city sexton, and market master. By 1895 the following were added: sanitary inspector, street commissioner, sergeant of police, resident physician, matron of the hospital, pound master, bridge keeper, city auditor, and porter.[24]

The methods of selecting these city officials varied from time to time. According to the 1878 charter, the treasurer, marshal, attorney, assessor and collector, and the city engineer were all elected at large,[25] while the clerk, physician,

---

23 Ibid., P. 284.
24 Minute I, Sept. 2, 1895, P. 235.
25 Robertson, op. cit., Art. 403, P. 121.

23

and sexton were appointed by the mayor. Later the board of aldermen chose the city officers.[26] It was not until the latter years of the mayor-aldermanic government that all major officers were elected at large by the Austin electorate. Their terms of service corresponded to those of the aldermen and mayor. When aldermen served two-year terms, so did the administrative officers.

Much of the administrative work of the city during the last half of the nineteenth century was under the supervision of advisory or administrative boards or committees, responsible to the mayor or the board of aldermen. For instance, in 1861 a board of health was established composed of five physicians, with the city physician serving as chairman, which had regulatory powers to enforce the city's health ordinances. Later the board of appraisers and equalization was created with power to make corrections in tax assessments. In 1890 the board of public works was brought into existence. This board was charged with the responsibility of building and operating the hydroelectric plant and was responsible to the board of aldermen. Later its name was changed to the water and light commission and made a standing committee of the board. Finally, in 1897 the water and light system was placed under the control of four water and light commissioners, all of whom were directly elected by the voters. Shortly before the later date, the board of street and sewers, composed of five citizens appointed by the board, was created with the responsibility to recommend to the aldermen plans for street and sewer construction and repair.

These are but a few of the many illustrations that could be given to demonstrate the lack of centralized administrative control which existed in Austin under mayor-aldermanic government around 1900.

Although the mayor was looked upon as being the city's chief administrative officer he was without power to pre-

---

26 *American Statesman*, Sept. 16, 1880.

pare its budget. This was done by the board. He did possess the item veto power, but as we have seen, this was used primarily as a threat — an ax over the head of the legislative body.

In the early period before city judges and courts were established as a separate branch of municipal administration, the mayor held forth as Austin's chief magistrate. He held mayor's court each morning, where all misdemeanor cases involving city regulations were tried. He had criminal jurisdiction delegated to him by both the city charter and state statute. Essentially, he served an overlapping jurisdiction with the justice of the peace.[27]

Acting as a judge in these cases, the mayor demonstrated all of the essential powers of a trial judge. He could issue warrants for arrest, summon witnesses, grant new trials or postpone them, and could fine persons for contempt of court.[28] The mayor served in this judicial capacity until 1886, when the office of city recorder was established by charter. The city recorder served the role of municipal judge.[29] The mayor had the power to perform marriage ceremonies.

Growth -- Inefficiency -- Reform

The dominant characteristics of Austin's city government during the last half of the nineteenth century all hinged around the democratization of city hall. The mayor and aldermen were elected for short terms and reelection was on the whole infrequent. The board of aldermen was large and elected by wards. The mayor shared his administrative powers with the governing body committees and popularly elected administrative officials. The administra-

27 Robertson, op. cit., Art. 374, P. 115.
28 Ibid., Art. 364, P. 113; Art. 370, P. 114; Art. 371, P. 114.
29 Ruggles and Johnson, op. cit., Art. X, P. 22.

tion was hydra-headed and it was impossible to fix responsibility on any one person. The political theory of the period demanded rotation in public office. All this made for little stability, a lack of efficiency in administration, and high taxes for the citizens.

For the two or three decades following the Civil War, Austin's government sank to low levels. During this period inefficiency was the order of the day, corruption and graft were common and the public for the most part appeared indifferent. They accepted the situation with little protest. The local newspaper was not too concerned and was frequently accused of promoting the ends of the Democratic party — effective civic leadership was lacking.

Throughout this period Austin's financial problems never ceased; the city's bonded indebtedness skyrocketed to a point at times when it exceeded the limits set by the state constitution. This led to excessive interest rates and higher taxes. While city hall struggled with these problems their only answer seemed to be more revenue.

The development and providing of public utilities for the city during the eighties, nineties, and early nineteen hundreds only added to Austin's critical problems. The building of the dam across the Colorado River and the difficulties related thereto were enormous; providing water, sewerage, and electricity to the city led to untold discussions and accusations; and the debate of private ownership of utilities vs. municipal ownership was not decided for years. The granting of franchises or permits to do business to street railway companies, ice companies, and gas works added additional opportunities for mismanagement and misuse of the public trust. The Austin citizen paid dearly for these services during this period.

It was said that the taking and giving of bribes was not unknown and that persons seeking special favors from the city often paid for the privileges they desired. The marshal and police officers were at times accused of distributing, illegally, poll tax receipts; election judges were charged with improper conduct; and various other misuses were said to have occurred at the ballot box. The citizens at last became suspicious of their city officials and the officials distrusted each other. The complete accusations and the names of all those involved were not recorded in the official journal; neither were the reports of the committees appointed by the board to investigate these charges. While the board of aldermen did hold hearings to study the cases, after much delay and repeated postponements, all seemed to have acquitted the city officials involved.

A number of factors combined to produce this unwholesome state of affairs. The form of government with its responsibility divided among mayor, aldermen, administrative officials and committees, some of them popularly elected, some chosen by the mayor and aldermen, made it impossible to place responsibility on anyone for the things that went wrong. Again, the last half of the nineteenth century were prosperous years compared with those which had preceded them. The city was growing and property values were going up. At the same time the demand for city services was multiplying. Activities that had formerly been left to private initiative were coming to be regarded as falling within the sphere of government. Also, it was during this period that such functions as public health began to receive more of the city's attention. The city began to provide more services, employ more people, and spend more money. It is little wonder that graft and maladministration were common. The spoilsmen were more active because the spoils were greater.

As matters went from bad to worse the smoldering resentment of the people began to burst into the open. The public commenced to tire of incompetents in public office and the tune changed from "to the victor belong the spoils" to "to the competent belong the jobs." Austin citizens began to petition the city fathers about their grievances, outstanding civic leaders like M. M. Shipe, Louis Hancock, A. P. Wooldridge, Judge Charles Rogan, Will H. Cullen, James

P. Wallace, W. L. Vining and others expressed their complaints about the city's mismanagement and corruption. The Business League, led by these men and composed of a group of businessmen-reformers, came into being.

In 1901, Austin citizens became dissatisfied to the point that the board of aldermen was reorganized. The twenty-two-member board was pared to fourteen; however, this change did not bring about responsible government in the city.

The Business League launched a campaign to change the form of government and to adopt one more in keeping with the times. They wished to take politics out of government. The emphasis was to be placed on "openness and a form of government which fixes the individual responsibility of mismanagement or malfeasance in the office."[30] It was their contention that by placing city affairs in the hands of a small group of men, five or seven, skilled in business management, city government would be made directly responsible to the people and in this way order would be brought to municipal affairs.

A new charter was drafted and when it was presented to the voters in 1909, Austinites approved it by an overwhelming vote of two to one.[31] A San Antonio paper in commenting on Austin's new form of government said, "An awakening of the capital city from that sleep which classed it with the unprogressive places of earth."[32]

The old regime was purged. The mayor, the aldermen and a host of city officers were swept into oblivion. City hall came under the control of a mayor and four commissioners, all elected at large, for a term of two years each.

Mayor-aldermanic government was perhaps effective in Austin for a period of years. But as the city grew, demands for services increased, those in control tried to meet these

---

30 *San Antonio Light and Gazette,* March 30, 1910.
31 Idem.
32 Idem.

needs by expanding the system. Additional municipal officers, more boards, and agencies were established. The result proved to be an inefficient, inoperable administrative unit directed by incompetent men. The unwieldy board of aldermen, unskilled in the methods of city management, was unable to cope with the pressing problems of finance and public service. At last the people spoke — they demanded a change in the machinery of government and the personnel who directed it. The commission form of government became a reality.

IV

Commission Government

EXCEPT FOR THE "INFANT YEARS" WHEN dedicated and capable men gave their time and energies in its behalf, the commission government in Austin proved to be little better than the government it had replaced.

Despite the new face of government and the promise of change, the inherent problems of combined legislative and administrative power were not solved, and gradually Austin was right back where she started, as the old political leadership was once more in power.

Changes in the form of government may be compared to an individual who does not seek the assistance of a doctor or dentist until he is forced to do so. A community is likely to tolerate a form of government until a catastrophe strikes such as a flood, a fire, a hurricane, a tornado, or a financial disaster. The failure to restore order and provide the necessary services so often is placed upon the machinery

30

of government rather than upon those who man the organization — where some of it rightly belongs.

In case of a crisis, good men tend to rush to the defense of their community. Some of them seek and are elected to office — the form of government may be varied or changed — both policy making and administration are improved for a while because of citizen interest and improved personnel at city hall. Finally, community interest subsides, mediocrity takes over the reins of government until another major crisis develops. It seems that we learn from history that we do not learn from history.

Galveston is sometimes credited with the origin of the commission form of city government in 1901. It would be more correct to say that Galveston advertised this form of government. As a matter of fact, the borough councils of colonial days were not radically different from the "Galveston Plan."

Houston adopted the commission plan with some modification in 1905, and by 1907 five other Texas cities fell into line; so did Des Moines and Davenport, Iowa. However, it was Des Moines which popularized commission government. The framers of the Des Moines charter took the Galveston charter and superimposed upon it initiative, referendum and recall, a nonpartisan ballot for primaries and elections, and a merit system. Thus, as more cities adopted commission government, it was the "Des Moines Plan" and not the "Galveston Plan" which came to be used. By 1917, the spread of commission government reached its peak, with five hundred cities using it. Since then the number has steadily decreased.

In Texas, between 1901 and 1915, most of the large cities secured special charters from the legislature providing for the plan. The legislature also made provision for the commission form in the general laws in 1909 and 1913. However, since 1915 home rule cities in Texas have gradually turned away from commission government; at the present time there are not more than two or three of them using

31

this form of government. Less than one-fourth of the general law cities continue to use the commission plan in Texas.

What Commission Government Is

One is not likely to find any two cities using commission government where all the details are alike. Nearly every city has made changes and modifications to meet its particular desires and local situation. But regardless of this lack of similarity in detail, the commission cities have much in common regarding their administrative organization. The number of elected commissioners varies from three to nine, five being the more common number; their terms of office range from two to six years, and their salaries vary greatly from city to city. Collectively this group constitutes the city council, but individually they serve as heads of the city's various departments. Thus, in a commission-governed city the commissioners serve in a dual capacity. As a group they compose the city's legislative body, formulating municipal policy, while individually they serve as administrative heads of the several departments.

The Galveston charter of 1901 did not contemplate that the administrative affairs of the city would be actually handled by the commissioners themselves. These individuals were to serve the city part-time, and were given the authority to appoint and discharge all employees, including department chiefs. The original Galveston Plan thus provided that appointed department heads were to serve the city under the supervision of the commissioners. This original concept was soon lost and various methods of assigning commissioners to head the departments rapidly came into use. The practice of permitting the commission to assign its members to head the departments became common. In a few instances these assignments are made by the mayor, while in a number of other cases the voters elect commissioners to head specific departments. There is a trend in the direction of the latter method today.

Unless one commissioner is excused from a departmental directorship to serve as mayor, the number of city administrative departments will correspond to the number of commissioners. Ordinarily the mayor is elected to a specific position. Some charters provide that the candidate receiving the highest number of votes will be mayor; in other cities the commissioners choose one of their own number to preside at commissioners' meetings and to serve as mayor. In commission government the position of the mayor is not an important one. He has no veto and usually is not able to make more appointments than do the other commissioners. As titular head of the city, he may be more influential than the other members, but his administrative and legislative powers are shared with them. His salary, however, may be slightly higher than that paid the other members.

Advantages

One advantage of the commission form of city government is that it is simple. Its two outstanding characteristics are:

1. A small commission, elected at large, which serves as the legislative body.
2. Each commissioner acts as head of an administrative department.

The proponents of the form claim that it attracts leading business and professional men to serve their city and that in this way it serves as a method of raising the prestige of public officeholding. It is unfortunate that experience and practice do not substantiate so many of the merits claimed for this form of government.

Defects

Commission government has been found to have most of the defects of the weak mayor form in addition to some of its own. One of its chief faults is that it makes no organizational distinction between the policy-making function of government and the administrative function. Most will agree that the qualifications are not the same for both the legislator and administrator. The running of a department within a large city requires a considerable amount of executive ability in addition to specialized information on the subject matter with which the department deals. A policy maker represents the citizens, and he should know what they expect of government. Under the commission form, elected officials perform both functions. They legislate for the city, and they are also in charge of the city's various executive departments. The elective process seldom brings to office men with great administrative talent. Personality, financial backing, and the support of a political organization are all necessary to produce votes. Many good administrators do not have these attributes. Furthermore, one who possesses the qualities of a successful administrator will rarely run for office under the conditions of the commission plan. He frequently will refuse to risk the uncertainty of tenure which every elective official faces.

In commission government no single commissioner has authority over his fellow commissioners in their administrative capacities. Whatever influence he may exercise over them is done in an extralegal capacity. All this means that there is no way of coordinating the activities of the city's various departments and agencies; there is no one with an overall view of the needs of these organizations, nor is there anyone to make quick decisions or to act quickly in case such is required. In case of error or misdeeds, both the legislative body and citizens alike are at a loss to know upon whom they are to fix the blame.

Someone once said that commission government is like a motorcar with an accelerator but no brake. When the men who vote the funds are the same men who spend them, the cost of government is not likely to be reduced. It is inevitable that each commissioner will ask for as much as he can get. If he is politically ambitious, he will naturally fight for more positions in his budget and will seek to have more contracts awarded in order that his sphere of influence be increased. The tendency is for the commissioner to spend, and there is no method made for reducing expenditures. The commission form provides no means of paring down budgets, despite the fact that experience teaches that most department heads ask for all they believe it is possible to get. It would seem that commission government gives full opportunity for the old principle of the pork barrel to operate.[1]

Austin Adopts Commission Government

After watching the apparent success of commission government in a number of other Texas cities and upon being plagued with the rigorous problems with water, light, and the streetcar company, a group of citizens headed by M. M. Shipe spent a greater part of 1908 attempting to convince the Austin voters that a change in the city charter providing for commission government would assist in finding a solution to their many municipal difficulties. On December 29, 1908 the Austin electorate by a vote of almost two to one accepted the commission form.

The Wooldridge Administration

The next step was the election of a mayor and commissioners to run the new government. On March 23, 1909 the first primary was held. When the votes were counted, A. P. Wooldridge led Frank R. Maddox in the mayor's race and the four men chosen for commissioners were E. C. Bartholomew, D. B. Gracy, James P. Hart, and P. W.

---

1 See Stuart A. MacCorkle, *American Municipal Government and Administration* (Boston, 1948), pp. 285-292.

Powell. On April 6, the runoff election date, Wooldridge and the four commissioners were unopposed.[2]

The mayor and commissioners were all men of experience and prominence in their community. A. P. Wooldridge was no doubt the best trained and most distinguished man to be elected mayor of Austin to the present day. He was well educated, being a lawyer by profession. His character was above reproach and in every respect he was a gentleman. Mr. Wooldridge was experienced and knowledgeable in many fields such as banking, education, and insurance. A warm personality and a cooperative understanding of people and their problems made him a leader of men. He was outstanding in both his private and public life — one who worked unselfishly for his city and his state.[3]

The four commissioners had won for themselves a place in the community. E. C. Bartholomew was a prominent banker and real estate man; David B. Gracy was in the abstract business and later vice-president of the Mutual Savings Institution when it was organized in 1920; James P. Hart was the Clerk of the 26th and 53rd Judicial District Courts and a long-time public servant in Austin; and Pinckney W. Powell owned a lumber and planing mill and was yardmaster for the International Great Northern.

These were the first commissioners chosen to serve under the new commission form of government in Austin.

The various functions of city government were divided among five departments:

First — The Department of Public Affairs, Mayor A. P. Wooldridge.

Second — The Department of Receipts, Disbursements and Accounts, Commissioner, D. B. Gracy.

Third — The Department of Parks and Public Property, Commissioner, E. C. Bartholomew.

---

2 *Austin American-Statesman*, April 6, 1909.

3 For an authoritative and well-written biography of A. P. Wooldridge see Ruth Ann Overbeck, *Alexander Penn Wooldridge*, (Austin, 1963), P. 74.

Fourth — The Department of Streets and Public Improvements, Commissioner, P. W. Powell.

Fifth — The Department of Police and Public Safety, Commissioner, James P. Hart.

When A. P. Wooldridge was sworn into office as mayor of Austin he made a written statement to the commissioners and the people of Austin which exemplified the character and the ability of the man who made them. The writer believes them so remarkable that excerpts of this speech are quoted below.

". . . When entering upon a new administration and upon the installation of a radically different form of government, it is usual and proper that the head of that administration and the chief representative of such new form of government should recall to his associates, and through them to the public, the things for which he and they stand and give briefly a statement of the causes leading to the substitution of the new for the old and state some of the distinguishing characteristics of this new form of government as contrasted with the old, and show wherein they are better.

"As we have had many conferences since our election, April 5, I have gotten to know your individual views as to the best general policies for Austin, as well as your particular plans and opinions for your special departments, and as our opinions are in entire agreement, much of what I shall hereafter state will be given to the public, not so much as my personal judgment alone as the collective thought of the entire council.

"In the old 'aldermanic' form of city government, which has been in practically universal use in the United States for the last hundred years and more, two features are prominent: The first is the election of local representatives from local constituencies principally for purely local purposes. The second is the diffusion of responsibility and consequent

37

accountability amongst a large number of persons —
amongst, say five to fifty persons, according to the size [of]
the boards of aldermen. A proper consideration of the large
interests of the entire city, and a responsibility to the
whole people is impossible under this form of government,
and when there is no close responsibility, experience has
shown there can be no guaranty high of efficiency [*sic*].

"Under our present form of government there are also
two prominent features — and they are in direct contrast
with the old form. The first is that each councilman is
chosen by the whole people and represents the whole people
and not a particular ward. And secondly, he is responsible
to the whole people and not to those alone of a particular
subdivision of the city, and his responsibility is direct and
personal. And it is this representation of the whole city
and this direct accountability to the whole people which
gives to the commission form of government its superiority
over the aldermanic form.

"Myself and yourselves are trustees for the whole city —
but we are also heads of special departments. We are given
large discretionary and administrative powers, both as a
whole body and in our special departments, and we will be
held responsible for results.

"As mayor, I am charged by the charter with a general
supervision over all of the affairs of the city. I shall take an
active but not an officious interest in the affairs of each of
your departments. I believe you cordially desire I shall do
this. I cordially invite your advice and assistance in the
conduct of my particular department. As an administration
we will be judged as a whole, but should any particular
department prove to be particularly strong or particularly
weak, the credit of success or the reproach of failure must
attach to the head of that particular department.

* * *

"Myself and yourselves were proposed to the voters of
Austin first by a committee of eleven persons and after-

38

wards by a mass meeting of about five hundred citizens. We were afterwards nominated at a public primary held on March 22, 1909, winning by majorities of 1,026 and downwards. On April 5, 1909, we were elected without opposition to our present positions as the first commissioners of Austin at about an equal vote of 1,660 persons.

"No one of us sought the office to which he has been called by the generous partiality of our fellow citizens. Our charter is nonpartisan and should be administered in the broadest sense of that word. I believe that personal merit rather than individual partisanship should be the standard with us of fitness for employment.

* * *

"For myself and associates in the exercise of our responsible trust I invoke the patient forbearance of our people and ask their active and persistent cooperation.

"Austin needs many things of a public character. She needs better streets, sidewalks, parks and sewers. And Austin has but little money in her treasury. If these things are to be accomplished for Austin her people must help, liberally help in the way of private contributions as well as through the medium of taxation.

"Our people must be warned against expecting much and too soon. It will be impossible for the new government to work miracles. It can only hope by economy and insistent energy to bring about a slow improvement in things. Our progress will be slow or fast just in proportion as our people will help, by their advice, their encouragement and their material aid.

"Above all things I invoke harmony amongst our people. Let the differences between us be forgotten and let us unitedly make common effort for our common good."[4]

A. P. Wooldridge served his city as mayor for four

---

4 *Austin Daily Statesman,* April 20, 1909.

successive terms, April 19, 1909 to April 30, 1919. He served the longest number of years in this position of anyone until his time. Nor were there many changes made in the personnel of the commission during this period. In 1911 Harry L. Haynes replaced David B. Gracy and in 1913 William B. Anthony took the place of James P. Hart.

During the Wooldridge administration the commission form of government seemed to run smoothly. Many improvements were made at city hall. For example, not only were a number of streets paved, but the method of doing so was made better. Much progress in the city's water and lighting systems was made and accurate records and plans for these services were installed. Mayor Wooldridge kept close to the pulse of Austin, but he was never afraid to move when he felt the city would be a better and more beautiful place by his doing so.

He was a man of much imagination and vision. He was a strong advocate for the establishment of the Austin Public Library and it was due to his influence that the state legislature was induced to grant the land for that purpose. Had it not been for World War I, no doubt the new permanent library would have been opened before March 1933. With the assistance of Dr. Herman G. James, Director of the Bureau of Municipal Research and Reference at The University of Texas, Mayor Wooldridge gave leadership and aided in the establishment of the Texas Municipal League. In 1913 at his invitation, all the cities in the state were invited to send delegates to Austin for an organizational meeting. Since that date the Texas League is among the strongest in the nation. Mayor Wooldridge was chosen to become its first president.

In 1917 Wooldridge advocated the partially completed Austin dam be finished. As a matter of fact, he predicted the Lower Colorado River Authority and its network of dams.

Perhaps to a greater extent than any other one man, Mayor A. P. Wooldridge labored for the good of his city — not for personal gain.

The mayor headed a "businessman's government" which took over the city, as we have seen, in 1909. The mayor's business position, his leadership, his untiring work and strong personality, brought honesty and efficiency to the city's municipal operations. This group believed that "He profits most who serves best," controlled city hall for the second decade of this century. It was composed of businessmen and civic leaders who took time off from their various activities to become the city's chief policy makers and top administrative officers. They were their own bosses; they were not politicians nor were they controlled by politicians — their chief object was the making of Austin a better place in which to live. To this end they dedicated themselves. They did the job themselves — they did not send errand boys to city hall to do their bidding.

The Yett Administration

Mayor Wooldridge declined to run again for office in 1919. Dr. W. D. Yett, a former state senator, a retired country doctor and rancher, became mayor, a position he held for six years. The only holdover commissioner from the previous administration was Harry L. Haynes. He was reelected in 1921 and again in 1923, thus serving during the entire period of the Yett administration, 1919-1925. The election of 1921 brought three new commissioners to city hall and the election of 1923 resulted in two new faces.

Apparently Mayor Yett was unable to impel the independent commissioners to run their departments with the welfare of the city as a whole in mind. The city seemed to show a lack of confidence in the municipal administration as an agency for community improvement. It consistently voted down bond issues that the administration wanted for badly needed public works. On all occasions it showed no inclination to grant the city the power to use the broader powers made possible by the recently adopted home rule amendment to the Texas Constitution.

41

While the commissioners were the heads of the administrative departments, the actual control seemed to be exercised by forces outside city hall. This so often happened when the city commission or council fell into mediocre hands. It is a truism that when any form of government is attacked, it is by the group who does not control it. No form of government is acceptable to all groups in the city. When businessmen give leadership and dominate government they are accused by the politicians as being undemocratic; and when politicians are in control they are attacked by businessmen as being corrupt and inefficient in the conduct of city affairs.

The citizens not only lost confidence in their government during the Yett administration but they lost interest in their community and seemed helpless to contribute to Austin's development. The following quotation on this subject perhaps carries more weight than any comment the author could make.

"The leading citizens of Austin, under the commission form of government, could see few ways in which their municipality served them, aside from the routine services such as police and fire protection and the maintenance of necessary utilities. Furthermore, they had few opportunities to serve their city government or participate in its affairs, unless they became active members of a political group or held a city job. It is not surprising that most of them left municipal problems to those who were willing to campaign for the commission offices and to deal with commissioners through political intrigue.

"The operation of a municipal library, for example, today enlists the participation in advisory capacities of leading citizens who are interested in the literary education and entertainment of the city. The recreation program now enlists the participation of citizens who wish to amuse themselves or render a social service. The commission government furnished neither service, and gave citizens no such opportunity to serve their city. The services that it furnished, such as police and fire protection and routine public works, encouraged a different type of citizen interest; the desire to sell materials to the city, to get a job from it, or to ask special exemptions from the law. In the absence of the present-day methods of citizen participation, the means of keeping citizens in touch with their government consisted largely of patronage, special favors, and personal intrigue. Under these conditions, interest in municipal affairs was not widespread, as was illustrated by the fact that the leading newspaper carried no article about the election of the last commission and mayor the day before that event occurred. The story of citizen participation in municipal affairs under Austin's commission government is mainly a negative one. The commission's contribution to the city's development, except for the period of Mayor Wooldridge's leadership, was negligible."[5]

5 Harold A. Stone, Don K. Price, Kathryn H. Stone, *City Manager Government in Austin* (Texas) (Public Administration Service), Chicago, 1939, pp. 6-7.

V

Council-Manager Government

ESTABLISHMENT OF THE COUNCIL-MANAGER form of government, popularly considered the "city manager form," is often a rocky experience for any municipality. Even after it has been established, this form of government is under periodic attack and criticism.

The other forms of municipal government are extremely political, and may be compared with the current organizations of county government in Texas. In these forms, political favoritism finds a fertile ground, and although there may be many instances of good public service, more often there are too many incidents of partisan decisions aimed at satisfying some particular political demands.

The city manager government, at least in its purest form, eliminates this probability. A professional manager, in charge of the city's income and expenditures, should be outside the political arena. Free from the pulls and tugs of this politician or that, he can operate the municipality

44

on a businesslike basis, obtaining the best service for the least tax dollar.

This situation, of course, sets him up as a target. Every temporary ill is laid at his doorstep; every ambitious politician may make him the villain of the community; every businesslike, but unpopular, decision may be assailed.

Thus, there are many cities operating under this plan that do not, in fact, have a "city manager form of government," for the simple reason that the mayor and councilmen do not allow the manager to do his job, while remaining in their own sphere of influence.

The lines of responsibility are clear, but become hazy on the days that the council meets. Austin has had a varied experience since adopting this form of government, probably not unlike that of other cities similarly situated.

At this writing, the future of this form of government in the Capital City may be considered to be in doubt.

If *father* means one who has begotten a child, the Supreme Being, God, creator, originator, or maker, then Richard S. Childs has no claim to being called "the father of council-manager government" as he and the National Municipal League, which he has dominated for years, are so fond of doing. To quote from a 1966 publication of The International City Management Association: "The need for professional city management was recognized as early as 1792 when George Washington wrote to Benjamin Franklin: 'It has always been my opinion . . . that the administration of the affairs of the Federal City ought to be under the immediate direction of a judicious skillful superintendent appointed by and subject to the orders of the commissioners.' "[1]

Many school boards had centralized administrative authority by appointing superintendents long before Prof.

1 *Council Manager Plan* (The International City Management Association, Chicago, 1966) P. 11. Also see Stuart A. MacCorkle, "Who Really Fathered the City-Manager Plan?", *One American City*, March 1966, pp. 106-107.

Charles E. Merrian of The University of Chicago unsuccessfully proposed a city executive be appointed by the city council at the Chicago Charter Convention in 1905. In 1908 Staunton, Virginia, by city ordinance, created the position of "General Manager" to be appointed by the council with full administrative duties. Staunton is the proud possessor of a plaque which now rests in her city hall honoring Charles E. Ashburner as the nation's first city manager. The plaque was a gift from The International City Management Association.

What Council-Manager Government Is

The identifying marks of the council-manager form are an elected council of citizens, who are responsible for policy making, and a professional chief administrator — the city manager — who is hired by, responsible to, and serves at the pleasure of the council, without a contract. The council is small, three to eleven members, and is generally elected at large, usually for a two- or four-year term. The council is responsible to the public for all policy making, and ultimately, for the quality of the overall city administration.

The mayor, in over half the cities in this country, is directly elected by the voters. In the remaining number, the council chooses one of their number to be the chairman of the council who is designated mayor of the city. Originally, in council-manager cities it was customary for the mayor to be chosen by his fellow councilmen. In more recent years, largely in response to popular demand for strong political leadership, there has been a trend toward separate direct election of the mayor. Austin, beginning in 1971, has followed this pattern.

The mayor presides over council meetings, serves as the city's ceremonial head, and in times of emergency, he may be charged with the duty of preserving order. He also serves as the city's political head. His compensation may be

46

higher than that of his fellow councilmen, and some charters give him additional powers. Freedom from administrative duties provides him time to give policy leadership to the city. The mayor, under this form of government, is in a position to effect compromises, evaluate public sentiment, and generate support for the city's policies and programs. The office is largely what he has the ability to make of it.

The most important duty of a councilman is decision and policy making. He should be a leader and well informed to vote on the various issues which come before the council. He should never lose sight of the fact that as an elective representative, he is responsible for the effective and responsive administration of the city's affairs.

The city manager's job, like that of a councilman, is complex. He is an administrator, a public relations man, a policy advisor, a planner, and a dollar stretcher. He might be characterized as the late English novelist W. L. George described an English civil servant: ". . . a man of oil, silver, and steel, capable of every delay and grace, suggestive of every sympathy and capable of none, incapable of a lie, always capable of an evasion, determined in public utility, yet not blind to private advancement, singularly addicted to justice, yet unable to suffer mercy. Not a man but a theorem, a diagram, a syllogism."

By and large, the city manager maintains much the same relationship to the council that the president of a university does to the board of regents, or as the manager of a business corporation does to the board of directors. In each case, there is a single administrator who is chosen and controlled by the board, to manage the affairs of the institution or the business according to the general policies established by the board. Council-manager government, therefore, is based upon tried and proven American business principles.

Opposition to the adoption of the manager plan in local referendum campaigns frequently is inspired by officeholders who take offense at the effort for the change as a reflection on their management or as an attempt to oust them and substitute a new group. The arguments commonly made are that "it is one-man power," "we don't want any out-of-town expert coming in here to run our government," "the city manager will be flitting away to a bigger town," "it's undemocratic not to elect the principal executive officer." These may be effective charges in a particular election contest, even though the answers are readily found in the actual experiences of council-manager cities.[2]

The manager and the council work as a team. A mutual respect and confidence must exist between them. A councilman cannot be an expert on all subjects, but he must know enough about the matters at hand to understand the problems; he must act responsively, responsibly, and in so doing, exercise good judgment. The manager's main function is to serve the council; he does the research and presents the facts — the council reviews, studies, revises and formulates policy. The manager implements the council's policy decisions.

The art of politics is the art of dealing with people. Both the council and the manager must be realists and politically sophisticated.

Council-Manager Government in Austin

When Mayor A. P. Wooldridge declined to seek re-election in 1919, no man of comparable ability stepped forward to give his time to the city affairs, with the result that city hall fell under the direction of men of mediocre ability.

With conditions continuing to worsen, Austin businessmen, with the able help of Walter E. Long, the secretary of the Austin Chamber of Commerce, assistance of a few individuals from The University of Texas such as Dr. Herman

---

2 See Stuart A. MacCorkle, *American Municipal Government and Administration* (Boston, 1948), Chapters XIII, XIV.

G. James who suggested the idea, and a local newspaper, the *American,* were largely responsible for Austin's adopting council-manager government by a majority of only 2,462 to 2,413 votes in 1924. Austin's estimated population at the time was approximately 42,000.

The members of the first council under the manager plan were men of some prestige in the community. Dr. P. W. McFadden, the owner of a pharmacy in the university area and president of a small local bank, was chosen by his colleagues to become the first mayor under the amended council-manager charter. A printing shop foreman, Victor Pannell, and D. C. Reed, a cotton broker, served on the council with Mayor McFadden from 1926 to 1931. An owner of a leather goods factory and retail store, Robert Mueller, and a lumber dealer, Ben Barker, served only one term. In 1927 these two were replaced by Leo O. Mueller, brother and partner of the former councilman, and E. L. Steck, the owner of an office supply factory and store, who remained on the council until 1933. Except for Mr. Pannell, these men were all on the board of the Austin Chamber of Commerce.[3]

The council which took office in 1926 was faced with the task of putting into operation a new form of government and of introducing a number of new city services. The machinery of government had to be reorganized, the employees were nervous and jittery, city records were lacking in many cases, and in other instances they did not reveal the city's true financial condition. The council hardly knew where to start or which way to turn, due to the many problems.

Being confronted with such a heavy work load, the council soon learned to delegate detail and administrative work to the manager, and also to ask the assistance of a number of advisory boards, which were appointed in such

---

[3] Harold A. Stone, Don K. Price, Kathryn H. Stone, *City Manager Government in Austin* (Texas) (Public Administration Service), Chicago, 1939, P. 31.

fields as library, parks and playgrounds, and public health. The council spent much time discussing problems and solutions before reaching a decision; however, after a program was agreed upon, it was left to the manager to put it into effect.

It appears that the first council under the manager plan regarded themselves as being directors of a corporation, who did not have direct obligations to their constituents. They seem to have considered themselves more or less an independent lawmaking body not directly responsible to the electorate.

Harmony prevailed between this council and the manager. They thought alike and they talked the same language. They were a team which tackled city problems in a systematic and energetic manner to which the people of Austin had been unaccustomed.[4]

If a community has a record of good government, it is because it has been blessed with men of vision and courage, men imbued with a zeal for the progress of the community in its positions of trust and responsibility. Austin during the early years of council-manager government had men of such calibre at the helm.

Mr. Adam Johnson, a successful manager of a local department store and a former army officer, became Austin's first city manager. It is said that even his worst enemies gave him credit for both honesty and efficiency in building an organization and administering city affairs. As one of his friends once said, "He was too honest to make even minor concessions to political expediency in his administering city affairs." Mr. Johnson is reputed as commenting on one occasion, "When the people got impartial and honest government, they found they did not want it!"

As one reviews Adam Johnson's years at city hall, he is reminded of the words of Abraham Lincoln when a group sought to dissuade him from finishing the war in 1864.

---

4 For a detailed account of Austin's city government see Ibid., pp. 31-36.

50

To quote, "I desire so to conduct the affairs of this administration that if at the end, when I lay down the reins of power, I have lost every other friend on this earth, I shall at least have one friend left, and that friend shall be down inside me."

Austin owes much to Adam Johnson. He gave council-manager government a firm foundation. In that day the city was fortunate in having a good machinery of government, as well as one that was well staffed.

The McFadden-Johnson administration was never close to the people. The council members seemed to care little about their own political fortunes. What they did care about was an efficiently run city government. The citizens were unaccustomed and unappreciative of such an approach to city administration. By and large, the voter will seldom tolerate an efficiently run city government for any great length of time unless he is continually reminded of the benefits which are being derived therefrom. This Mayor McFadden and his council failed to do.

For some six years the success of the businessmen's organization which had established council-manager government was wrought with few difficulties. But the business leadership of Austin, although capable of political activity on special occasions, was not dependable when routine political effort was needed. There was little or no opposition in the 1927 council election and none in 1929. But in 1931 and 1933, opposition appeared from candidates supported and led by Col. Andrew J. Zilker. Colonel Zilker had opposed the adoption of both the commission and the council-manager forms of government. In fact, his influence had affected political activities in Austin for years although he never held a public office.

New Leadership

In 1931, the businessmen's ticket won a majority of three of the five council positions, but in 1933 it lost four

51

members, the principal reason for the loss being the lack of interest on the part of council members themselves. Therefore in 1933, without organized support, without newspaper assistance, and with a lack of willingness on the part of incumbent council members to campaign in their own behalf, and because of the opposition that had been built up against Adam Johnson over the years, city hall passed back into the hands of the political leadership of Austin.

Two factors should be noted at this point. First, in 1933 and for the most of the years since that date, political leadership has come from inside the council itself. Second, business and professional men seem happy, for the most part, to have the politicians assume the burdens of public service so long as their interests are not endangered.

To return to the year of 1933 — it was then that Tom Miller first became mayor of Austin, a position which he held continuously at the will of the council until 1949 when he did not seek election. In 1955, he returned to city hall, remaining mayor until 1961, when he did not seek reelection because of ill health.

Mayor Miller was born in Austin where he spent his entire life. He was a successful businessman, owning a wholesale produce firm. Early in life he acquired a taste for politics and a love of history and the works of Shakespeare, whom he frequently quoted. He was willing to devote any amount of time and use his own personal resources to city affairs. He would hear anyone on any subject which concerned the city as long as that individual desired to speak.

The council which was elected with Miller in 1933, perhaps with a single exception, was experienced in local politics. Mr. Miller himself early became a staunch supporter of Pres. Franklin D. Roosevelt and the New Deal. Austin, it is recalled, constructed the first public housing unit in the nation in 1937, made possible by the Roosevelt administration. The close lines of communication and control between the Austin City Hall and Washington began in the early 1930s and still remains strong, though not perhaps as pronounced in recent years, partly because time has removed some of the players and others have departed the Washington scene.

Mayor Miller and his council, upon the resignation of Mr. Adam Johnson, chose Mr. Guiton Morgan as city manager. Mr. Morgan was trained as a civil engineer and had held administrative positions in both state and county governments, as well as having served for a brief period in private industry. The two men complemented each other well. As a matter of fact, the Miller-Morgan team only terminated after sixteen years when Mayor Miller did not seek reelection.

The council under the Miller-Morgan administration was relieved of actual managerial responsibility and was free to participate in the politics of city government. The manager considered it his duty to keep the council informed, in order that it answer to the people. He believed that the council's function was to keep the people friendly with city administration. Mr. Morgan never thought of himself as exercising his authority as a legal right — to him it was a delegated power. He once said, "I have the same relation to the council that one of my department heads has to me. It is the source of my authority."[5]

Stone, Price and Stone well characterized council-manager relations during this period in these words, "The Council, in short, now thinks its job as that of representing the public in dealing with the manager, and representing the government in dealing with the public. It thinks of the manager as merely its agent, but it does not act only as his board of business directors — it is his advertising department, his committee of public relations, and the coordinator of the lobbyists with whom the administration must deal. This relationship between the present council and manager has made a conspicuous change in attitude of the people

[5] The author was a member of the Austin city council during Mr. Morgan's last years at city hall.

towards the government. The manager is no longer exposed to political attack. No one believes that he is a chief executive removed from popular control, and careless of public opinion. The mayor and council, elected representatives, are given the credit and blame for even petty details of administration, and by keeping their ears to the ground as only politicians can, they retain the confidence of the public. . . . The present administration is clearly more likely to protect the manager from the attacks of political enemies, and his inconspicuous position makes him less subject to removal if other candidates defeat the present councilmen."[6]

Guiton Morgan served Austin as city manager from June 1, 1933 to June 1, 1950 except for the periods when he was on leave serving in the military. James A. Garrison was appointed acting manager during the first of these absences for a period of about six months in 1940-1941. During the second, April 14, 1942 to August 9, 1945, Walter E. Seaholm served as acting manager until Morgan's return to city hall.

Throughout this period of approximately eighteen years, Austin's government ran rather smoothly, despite the fact that these were among both the depression and war years. Austin's political and administrative leadership was, by and large, capable and dedicated to providing the citizens necessary municipal services at reasonable tax outlay. And it was to city hall that the citizen took his complaints and sought relief.

Austin during this period was not governed badly.

A Changing Era

Beginning in 1949 Austin had a series of one-term mayors. They followed in rapid order: Taylor Glass, 1949-1951; William S. Drake, Jr., 1951-1953; Charles McAden, 1953-1955. They were all able businessmen, Mr. Drake

---

6 Stone, Price, Stone, op. cit., pp. 43-44.

54

being president of Austin's largest privately owned enterprise at that time. None of them were professional politicians and each, after he had performed what he considered his civic duty, voluntarily returned to private life. During their terms of office, as in the case of Mayor Miller's numerous terms, municipal decisions were made, by and large, inside city hall.

Tom Miller returned to city hall in 1955 serving this time as mayor for a period of three terms. In all, he held this position for approximately twenty-two years. His term of service in this position is not only the longest in Austin's history, but it is marked by the fact that during his time he was the city's political head, as well as one of its outstanding business leaders.

Mayor Lester E. Palmer followed Mayor Miller's second stint at city hall, serving as mayor for the period 1961-1967. He had served as mayor pro tem during the latter years of the second Miller administration. The Palmer years at the city's helm may be best described by saying that leadership returned, for lack of a better word, to normalcy. The business community as a whole, and various other groups, took a greater part in the decisions made regarding the city than they had done in previous years — controls tended to move out of city hall. Austin had growing pains during the period, but the flood did wash away the dam.

From 1950 to 1967 Austin had two city managers. The first of these was Walter E. Seaholm who graduated in electrical engineering from The University of Texas in 1920. He came to Austin early in life and served this city for a number of years as its Director of Utilities. Beginning in April of 1942, he became acting city manager, serving for approximately three years, during the absence of Guiton Morgan. Upon Mr. Morgan's resignation, he was appointed manager on June 1, 1950, serving in this position until February 9, 1955.

The second manager in the period was W. T. Williams,

55

Jr. who was trained in law, holding a degree from The University of Texas. With the exception of military service he had at the time of his appointment spent his time in private practice and in the employment of the City of Austin, either in the Legal Department or the Tax Department. For a brief period he served as Assessor and Collector of Taxes, and at the time of his appointment to the manager's position, he was city attorney.

During this period of some sixteen years, few changes were made in the way things were done. With a few exceptions, the various city departments remained intact and under the direction of the same personnel. Austin did not seek outside administrative talent. As a matter of fact, from the beginning of council-manager government, Austin had relied largely upon homegrown administrators. The manager's job centered primarily on "line functions" and not "policy issues." These managers were all men dedicated to their communities and to their immediate job — they had little or no aspiration to someday manage a large city. This was also true of most department heads.

The mayor and council are exhibit number one at city hall. Any administration mirrors its council. Granting there has been a number of exceptions, it seems fair to say that looking back over the years, Austin's city councils have not taken any great interest in or shown a real leadership in the various professional municipal organizations, be they national or state. The council attitude has no doubt influenced the administrative staff to some degree. At the same time, one does not have difficulty pointing out a number of new administrative techniques and professional ideas that have been instituted during the period.

Austin's political leadership during most of the period could not be described as being aggressive. In 1953 the charter of the City of Austin was amended so as to require those seeking election to the council to announce for one of the five places on the council. Heretofore, a candidate announced for the council and the five receiving the highest number of votes were declared elected. The change may have affected the type of individual desiring to serve his city.

Also beginning in 1920, Austin witnessed a rapid population growth — an increase from approximately 35,000 at that time to an estimated number of 275,400 persons on January 1, 1972. Austin's economic growth, too, during the last twenty years, has been one of the best in the nation. For the first time, total assessed property valuations exceeded one billion dollars.

As a matter of fact, Austin's population and economic growth was so rapid during the last two decades that city government found it difficult to provide the bare necessary municipal services. The extra benefits were left undone. And during all this time Austin's social structure was changing. New people came with different and sometimes novel ideas and brought with them demands upon city government unknown to the earlier periods. Many seemed to think there had been a "caretaker government" at city hall too long.

In the spring of 1967 Harry Akin was chosen mayor and Mrs. Emma Long, a veteran of some sixteen years on the council, became mayor pro tem. Robert A. Tinstman, the first out-of-town manager in Austin's history, took office on September 1, 1967. Prior to his coming to Austin, Tinstman had been manager of Oklahoma City. Despite much fanfare, a great deal of publicity and many promises, little was done to improve municipal services to the people. Controls gravitated more and more into the hands of a limited number of politicians and their friends who were unable to return the mayor and his council to office in 1969.

Travis LaRue, a veteran of six years on the council, took over as mayor of the first seven-man council under council-manager government to serve Austin on May 15, 1969. Only one of this group, Ralph Janes, Jr., besides Mayor LaRue had served on the previous council. None

57

of them were politicians and a majority believed that decisions affecting the city should be made inside city hall. Controls moved back to the city hall and, some say, away from the people.

By 1969, Austin's governmental structure had grown unwieldy. There was a lack of coordination between the various agencies and departments of city government. Each department appeared to be operating as a separate and independent unit; thirty departments or agencies were reporting to the city manager. Austin's government was more or less operating on a day-to-day route basis. The council lacked strong political leadership and that which existed in the community was orientated towards private gain and personal glory.

These were some of the elements which existed in the Austin community and city hall when Lynn H. Andrews took over the manager's office on November 15, 1969. Prior to his Austin assignment, Andrews had been city manager of both San Antonio and St. Petersburg, Florida, serving in the latter city for approximately eight years.

It is doubtful if any city administration, in a two-year period, achieved so much toward improving administration and bettering services to the citizens of Austin. It is also perhaps true that in no two years did city hall receive so much criticism, or the citizens of the community receive less unbiased information as to what took place at city hall.

Some of this fault may justly be placed at the council's own doorstep. None of them were professional politicians and few of their number courted the news media. The council as a whole did not seek credit; it played to no individual or group; it was not in bed with anyone and apparently was willing to stand on its record of achievements.[7]

Any long-term public officeholder knows it is far safer, politically, for those in power to keep feeding the populace

---

7 For a detailed description of this period, see Stuart A. MacCorkle, "Two Years at City Hall," *Austin American-Statesman*, April 25, 1971; also *The Austin American*, August 26, 1971.

ideas and making promises than it is to take action. Unfortunately, efficient government is usually considered something for conversation or is happening elsewhere. There are very few who really want honest and efficient government.

Mayor LaRue and two of his councilmen, Jay L. Johnson, Jr. and D. R. Price, sought reelection in the spring of 1971. They were all unsuccessful.

The present city council may claim a number of firsts for Austin. As far as the writer is able to ascertain, this is the first time in Austin's history that a completely new council has been chosen — no member of the previous council was returned — Mr. Dick Nichols had served one term, 1967-1969. Second, Mayor Roy Butler is the first directly elected mayor to serve under the council-manager form of government. Third, Dr. S. H. Dryden is the first physician to serve under the council-manager form. Fourth, Mr. Berl Handcox is the first black to serve on the council since reconstruction days. Fifth, Mr. Lowell Lebermann is the first physically handicapped individual to serve Austin as a councilman. He is blind.

Again, with the present mayor and council, the controls have been removed from inside city hall. Fundamentally, the same power structure, with a few appendages added here and there, is in control today that took over the reins of government in the early 1930s and has held control for most of the time since then. The LaRue administration was one of the few exceptions to the rule. True, today the characters are different, times have changed, the tune has varied, but the end is the same economic and political group controls. However, these lines of control have been extended over the years until at the present time they include, in addition to the City of Austin, the state,[8] The University of Texas at Austin, and the Austin Independent School District. All more or less are inter-

---

[8] The election of 1972 will bring some changes here.

twined and interwoven in a master web. The same power structure controls all.

It might well be asked if council-manager government exists in Austin today. The mayor and council which took office on May 15, 1971, apparently have forgotten that Austin has a home rule charter. There seems to be no administrative detail too minute for their active participation. They glory in stating on numerous occasions, "We are running the city now."

City Manager Lynn Andrews submitted his resignation in early March which became effective June 2, 1972.

VI

The Council

CITY GOVERNMENT BEGINS WITH AN ELEC-
tion of the mayor and council members, and the three forms
of government for Austin have been built upon the duties,
powers and responsibilities of this elected body.

Some say that the council of today has fewer powers
than the councils under the two previous types of government. However, it is policy that establishes power, and the
council of today is the policy-making body of Austin, just
as all councils since the establishment of the city in 1839.

The quality of the government which exists in the community is in large measure dependent upon the calibre of
the elected representatives. These officials are selected by
the voters to represent them and to speak for them. Because
they have been so selected, they are looked to for leadership.

Any discussion of the city council quite naturally depends upon the period, the place, and the form of municipal government which is in operation at the time. Policy

61

determination is a legislative function and should be consigned to the city council. Today city councils, by and large, come nearer to performing this function than before. Especially this is true of those forms of municipal government which have developed since 1900 and have emphasized the importance of the council.

Under the commission plan all municipal powers are vested in the council or commission, which both formulates and carries out policy. The council-manager plan gives the council no direct control over administration, but provides that the chief executive be appointed by the council and solely responsible to it. The council oversees administration, but does not actually take part in its execution.

Both the commission and the council-manager forms of government provide for a small, one-house council. As a matter of fact, Austin has never operated under a bicameral council, regardless of the form of government in operation.

Size of the Council

Austin's first city council under the mayor-aldermanic or mayor-council system was composed of a mayor and eight aldermen. Apparently during the 1840s and early 1850s the number was decreased to six aldermen and a mayor, but by the late 1850s through the 1860s there were eight aldermen and the mayor. In the 1870s the number was ten and the mayor; in 1883 — twelve and a mayor; by 1890 the council was its largest — twenty-two and a mayor. However, shortly afterwards it dropped back to seven aldermen and the mayor, and in 1903 the board was again increased to fourteen plus the mayor, at which number it remained until 1909 when the form of government was changed.

Under the commission form of government Austin had four councilmen and a mayor. This same number was retained when council-manager government was adopted in 1926 and this number remained until 1967 when the charter was amended increasing the number to six councilmen and the mayor.

There seems to be a feeling that a comparatively small council will do better work and waste less time than a large one. While a council should not be unwieldy, it should be large enough to provide adequate popular representation. Various economic, geographic and social groups should be represented. In the opinion of the author, it seems that since the coming of the council-manager plan, Austin councils have been very representative of the community's life.

Term of Office and Remuneration

Under the mayor-council plan the term of office for the mayor and councilmen was one year. This seems to have been true until the mid-1870s when the term of office became two years. No remuneration was provided for the mayor and councilmen under this form of government until the seventies.

With the adoption of the commission plan, the mayor was paid $2,500 and each commissioner $2,000 per year — all were elected every other year. When Austin changed to council-manager government, the two-year term was retained, with elections being held for all members every other year and no salary was provided until May 15, 1967 when an ordinance was passed providing for $10 expenses for each councilman per meeting with a limit of fifty-two meetings per year. This allowance is still in force today.

The once popular theory that every person should give freely of his time and talent, with no reward save the joy of public service, has for the most part been abandoned. Within recent years, in other cities, there has been some tendency to increase the salaries of councilmen. Certainly some stipend should be paid if there is to be representation from all classes, because the individuals whose incomes are in the lower brackets are not in a position to donate their services entirely free.

Qualifications

The type of person elected to city councils varies greatly from city to city and from time to time within the same city. This is true, although charters and statutes alike attempt to standardize the type of candidate to be chosen by setting up formal requirements. But a number of qualifications can never be written into either charters or statutes. For instance, one of the most important attributes of a councilman is his interest in the city and its civic affairs. He must have a genuine, unaffected, and driving interest in the affairs of the community, without regard for the desires of isolated or particular groups who attempt to influence him for their own betterment. *Western City* expresses the idea well:

> A term as a member of a City Council . . . can be a rich and varied experience for a man. A certain amount of education is required, not formal learning, but a sense of the eternal fitness of things and of proper proportions, which is a mark of true education. A legislative official or one who sits upon the directorate for some particular municipal function, need not have any great accumulation of factual knowledge concerning the administration of government. But he does need judgment. He needs judgment to fit the immediate problem into its proper perspective. He needs to be sensitive to the countless problems which face him, and all of us, in this world in which we live today. He sits in a position of authority and power on questions of social interrelationships and personal interests, fully as often as he must make policy determinations on matters of public safety to water supply. Discrimination, tolerance, and ability to distinguish the sham from the genuine, a tough hide and a certain persistence toward a high

64

standard of decency in government — these are the qualities needed in a Councilman, regardless of the size of the city he serves.[1]

The Austin city charter requires that a councilman be at least twenty-five years of age at the time of his election, a citizen and qualified voter of Texas, a resident of the city for not less than three years next preceding his election, a taxpayer in the city, and not in arrears in the payment of any taxes or other liability due the city. A member of the council ceasing to reside in the city during the term for which he is elected immediately forfeits his office.[2]

In addition, certain negative qualifications appear; the councilman, for example, can hold no other office under the city government, or cannot be interested in any contract, work, or franchise which must be paid by the city. In most cases a councilman is forbidden to be surety for any person holding a contract with the city which may require security, or to be surety on a bond for any city officer.

Methods of Electing Councilmen[3]

There are a number of methods of choosing members of the city council. It may be done by election by wards, election at large, by a combination of the two foregoing plans, and election at large after nomination by wards. Our discussion here does not include proportional representation and preferential voting.

Where the ward system is used, the city is divided into areas which are supposed to be approximately equal in population, and each of these elects one or more councilmen. Wards or districts are arbitrary divisions, and their

---

1 *Western City*, Vol. XV, No. 1 (January 1939), P. 11.

2 *Charter of the City of Austin*, Art. II, Sec. 2, (1953).

3 See Stuart A. MacCorkle, *American Municipal Government and Administration*, (Boston, 1948) Chapt. XI.

boundaries may be altered from time to time by the council as the population of the city changes. When ward lines are disregarded and councilmen are chosen by the voters of the entire city, they are said to be elected at large. Election by wards is said to secure a better cross representation of the city. The gold coast, the poorer wards, the minority sections, and all others have a better opportunity to secure representation in the council under the ward system than where all are elected at large. Thus election by wards helps to secure representation of minority groups and also keeps the council in closer touch with the people. The ward system gives the voter a short and simple ballot. It has a tendency to place in the councilmen who may be presumed to know the needs of their respective localities.

Both methods have something to be said in their favor; on the other hand, both have their weaknesses. The ward system discourages men of broad vision who are able to see beyond the boundary of any given ward and understand the needs of the entire city. It places local whims above the general welfare and fosters a spirit of localism, for any councilman who owes his election to one ward will almost inevitably make its interest his own. His chief object will be to obtain the largest number of advantages in the way of public improvements for the ward which elected him, and he is generally safe so long as he succeeds. He will be inclined to help his fellow councilmen to get something for their wards, for in so doing he obtains their assistance in getting what he wants for his own. Thus, the work of the council often degenerates into a melee of trading and logrolling.

The ward councilman is usually a ward politician. When each ward is required to elect a representative, some able individual may be excluded from the council because he happens to live in the wrong neighborhood. If the ward system is used, a number of inferior men may be chosen because their districts are able to furnish no strong competition. Small districts are able to furnish no strong com-

66

petition. Small districts may mean the election of "small" men.

Election at large helps to attract better men to run for office; it encourages them to take a broader view on civic problems; and it places the council in a better position to reflect the sentiment of the entire community. By and large it tends to raise the whole calibre of the council, for in order to be selected by the whole community, an individual must have more than the favor of his immediate district. These are all arguments for the system, but there are items on the debit side which should be considered. Election at large virtually assures the majority party of a clean sweep at the polls. The minority group or groups are denied a real chance of electing a single candidate. The ward system is often criticized because it fails to give the minority party representation in proportion to strength, but election at large is open to the more serious criticism that it generally cuts the minority off from all representation. Not only are all the councilmen likely to belong to a single party, but they all may be chosen from one section of the city. However, the danger that any district will be neglected is not great, for each group generally is careful to draw its nominees from all parts of the city and from all classes. It would be poor policy to do otherwise. A real defect of election at large is that it increases the cost of electing the council because every candidate must conduct a city-wide campaign. The larger the community to be reached, the more the cost of the election.

A number of cities have experimented with other methods of electing their councilmen by combining the methods of election at large and by wards. In some cases this has been done by electing a part of the members by wards and the others at large. Kansas City, for example, elects approximately half of its council at large and the other half by wards. The same is true of Buffalo, Dallas, Houston, and Rochester.

Another plan which seeks to secure the advantages of

67

both methods is that of electing the councilmen at large but providing that they must live in the wards they represent. Atlanta, Georgia and Louisville, Kentucky both have plans similar to this. In California, Indiana, and North Carolina there are a number of cities where councilmen are nominated by wards but are elected at large.

Approximately sixty-five to seventy percent of the council-manager cities have councils chosen entirely at large. A sizeable number of council-manager cities have combined representation at large and by wards. Austin elects her mayor and six councilmen at large.

Apparently in 1863 under the mayor-council form Austin elected its councilmen by wards and continued this method of election until 1909. Since the latter date councilmen have been elected at large.

Vacancies

When a vacancy occurs on the council it is filled by a special election; however, if the vacancy is within ninety days of a regular election, no special election is called unless there is more than one vacancy. In case a runoff election is necessary it is held in the same manner as is provided in the charter for regular elections.[4]

Council Organization and Procedure

When a new council has been elected, its first duty is to meet and organize. In Austin this is done at its first meeting following each regular election of the mayor and councilmen. The mayor who is directly elected presides at all council meetings and is recognized as the head of city government for ceremonial, military, administrative purposes, and the receiving of civil processes. He is en-

---

4 *Charter of the City of Austin*, Art. II, Sec. 3, P. 6.

titled to vote on all matters considered by the council, but has no veto power. The council chooses one of its own number as mayor pro tem who acts as mayor during the absence or disability of the mayor.

The council also appoints the city clerk and such assistants as the office may need. In addition to the officers mentioned above it is customary for the city attorney and the city manager to be present at council meetings. Also, heads of the various departments are called in from time to time.

By charter the Austin city council is required to meet in regular session at the municipal building at least once each week, at such time as may be prescribed by ordinance, unless otherwise ordered by the council. Special meetings may be called by the city clerk upon written request of the mayor or three council members. Except for meetings where personnel matters are discussed, land acquisitions considered, matters wherein attorney-client privilege relationships are involved, and matters affecting security, all meetings must be open to the public.

The council by ordinance determines its own rules and order of business. Four or more councilmen constitute a quorum and no council action has any force unless it is adopted by the vote of four or more councilmen. Minutes of all council meetings are recorded and they constitute a public record.

The work of the city council may be performed at least in part through council committees. There are both standing and special committees. The number and their use have varied from council to council and from time to time, as has their method of appointment. For the most part Austin seems to have made little use of the committee system since the turn of the century.

Any councilman may introduce an ordinance. However, it must be in written form and related to but one subject. Before the ordinance is adopted the city attorney must approve it in writing or file his written objection with the city clerk. No ordinance can be passed on the day it is intro-

69

duced, unless it is an emergency measure and passed by a unanimous vote or a vote of three-fourths of the council. The charter provides that an ordinance shall not take effect until the expiration of ten days following the date of its final passage, except where the ordinance relates to the immediate preservation of the public peace, health, or safety, and is adopted as an emergency measure with a statement of the nature of the emergency.[5]

The Austin charter also requires that the city clerk shall give notice of the enactment of every penal ordinance and of every other ordinance required by law or this charter to be published, by causing the descriptive title or caption of the same to be published at least one time within ten days after final passage thereof in some newspaper or general circulation in the city.[6]

Powers of the Council

The policies of the city council are generally expressed through the enactment of ordinances and resolutions. A city ordinance is the lowest grade of legislation in our legal hierarchy. It must not be in conflict with the federal Constitution, treaties, federal statutes, executive orders, state constitution, state statutes, or the city charter. The municipal corporation has only those powers which are specifically authorized or implied. As a general rule, its authority has been rather strictly construed by the courts.

On the exercise of the powers granted to the municipal corporation, the council holds an important position. The Austin city charter gives and the courts have held that powers granted to the city and not conferred upon any particular officer belong to the council. On the other hand the Austin charter prohibits the council taking certain

---

5 Ibid., Art. II, Sec. 11, pp. 8-9.
6 Ibid., Art. II, Sec. 12, P. 9.

actions; for example, interference in personnel matters, or the selling, leasing and mortgaging of dedicated park land, unless approved by the qualified voters of the city.

The council not only formulates policy, but it has the responsibility to see that the policy is carried out. The council passes the budget, it fixes the tax rate, it incurs debts, it makes contracts, it annexes and zones territory and the like. The power of doing all these things and seeing that they are done correctly is the council's responsibility.

Knowing what to do at times is not so difficult as getting it done. The latter is an art. Every councilman soon realizes that he can get little done alone. He needs the assistance of his colleagues; he learns the importance of delay, but at the same time he must not stall too long. As a former mayor of Austin often said, "Planning is the art of timing." A councilman must rely on the administrator, for, as a policy maker, he is asked to pass on all types of problems — from the issuance of bonds to the installation of one-way streets. He must consult the manager and his department heads. He is well advised in having these individuals suggest policy on legislative matters. An old-time reporter may sometimes be the best senior member on the council. Austin has not been so blessed since the days of William J. Weeg and Paul Bolton.[7]

The council, as we have said, is primarily a legislative body, but its control over administration is by no means slight. It appoints and removes the city manager at will. The council appoints the city clerk and the assistants who serve in that office, the judges of the corporation court, the clerk and deputy clerks of this court, and members of various advisory boards and commissions, such as the Board of Equalization, the Library Commission, the Advisory Hospital Board, the Planning Commission, the Parks and Recreation Board, the Navigation Board, the

---

7 See Stuart A. MacCorkle, "A Professor Becomes a Councilman," *Texas Municipalities*, Vol. XXXVII, No. 8, pp. 201-205.

Model Neighborhood Commission, the Solicitation Board, the Human Relations Commission, the Citizens Tax Advisory Commission, and others.

The council's function is to oversee administration, but not to become hopelessly involved in the details of the administrative process. It should never become immersed in a labyrinth of trifling affairs which only a competent administrator can dispose of efficiently. The council's primary duty is not to execute policy. This is an administrative function.

The Austin city charter gives the council the power to grant franchises covering the use of city streets and other property. Some of the more common of these are: gas companies, telephone companies, bus companies, airlines, and other businesses requiring the use of city property. The city council may also enter into many contracts involving the city, such as providing for the erection of public buildings, the renting of buildings, equipment, and providing of services or the buying or selling of city property, thus exercising administrative powers of considerable importance.

In the charter, the council has the power to create new departments or agencies which shall be under the control of the city manager. Likewise, it may abolish any department not created by the charter or create or combine one or more departments it creates, but before so doing it is required to first obtain and consider the recommendations of the city manager.

Summary

The city council is the custodian of the public interest in the locality. It should act to protect that interest. It cannot afford to expend its energies primarily on minor matters which only consume its time in endless deliberations. Instead it should direct itself to the basic problems of staff, finance, planning, fundamental law, future needs and programming.

The council role, especially in the council-manager form of government, is to assign to competent individuals or organizations, inside or outside the municipal organization, the staff work required, reserving to itself the function of review, coordination, and decision making, always with the public interest in mind.

A successful council, among other things, requires an understanding of the leadership structure of the community — including the political, business, social, religious, organizational, and the various "specialists."

The challenge to city councils today is to rise above the routine, seek competent assistance and come to grips with the major problems. An unsatisfactory system does not have to be accepted. Change is possible if sufficient energy is concentrated on the problem and its solution. However, it will require more than verbiage, news releases, and television appearances. Too many councilmen talk the problems to death, but few do anything about them.

Most city governments are run by men of rather ordinary talent and morality, which may well be attributed to the fact that we have a representative system of government. However, ever so often in most communities a man of unusual ability, intelligence, and integrity is elected to public office, who serves well and honorably his constituency. Austin has been fortunate in having a number of mayors and councilmen of such calibre. To single those out would be a hazardous if not an impossible task, but names like Edwin N. Waller, the first mayor of Austin; Mayor A. P. Wooldridge and the various councilmen who served with him through his three terms at city hall; Mayor P. W. McFadden and those who worked with him in establishing council-manager government on a firm basis in our capital city; Tom Miller and many of those who labored with him during his twenty-two years as mayor of Austin; these, and others, have given of themselves and extended their best

73

efforts to make their city great. They are proof that, in the words of James Madison, "We can depend on the capacity of mankind for self-government." It is regrettable that their kind seem to become more and more infrequent all the time.

Population growth, urbanization, and industrialization of life has had a profound impact upon the operation of political institutions in Austin, as has been true elsewhere. Changes have occurred in the strength and the structure of the local economic, political, and social elite. A growing middle class is showing its spurs, but in present-day Austin, the political leadership has converted the middle class and the poorer groups into supporting the established order. You cannot live on other people's promises, but if you promise others enough, you can live on your own for years. A rather recent local council member demonstrated this truism to the satisfaction of many Austin citizens.

Keeping the governmental structure strong and at the same time flexible enough to meet today's and tomorrow's problems is no small undertaking. Austin in 1969 followed the example of some other Texas cities using council-manager government and amended her charter so as to provide for the direct election of the mayor. And since coming to office in May of 1971 Mayor Roy Butler and the council placed seven positions in the budget for the purpose of serving as administrative assistants to the council.[8] To legalize the action these positions were placed in the city clerk's office. No attempt is made here to say whether these actions are good or bad — the fact is that they are steps towards decentralizing administration and reducing the powers of the city's chief administrative officer — the city manager. The spirit of the city charter has been negated.

It does not follow that leadership is necessarily inherent in the system of direct election. Experience does teach us this simple fact — council interference in the details of administration will wreck any system. Under such condi-

---

8 Councilman S. H. (Bud) Dryden has stated that he does not desire an administrative assistant.

tions it soon becomes not a system — but organized chaos. Employee morale deteriorates, competent staff members soon resign and seek positions elsewhere. The entire community suffers.

Someone has said, "Consistency is the virtue of fools." but when carried to the extreme and the council becomes a weather vane to the extent that it makes a decision one week only to return to city hall seven days later to reverse itself or alter its course of action, administration is brought to a standstill — government in its best sense ceases to exist. A mature council with good judgment and intestinal fortitude does not conduct its business in such a manner.

If our objective in Austin is not necessarily good government, but democratic government, then this attitude has been reflected in the type of councilmen serving the city over the years. Austin's councils have gradually become more representative of the people with the passage of time. People being the way they are and the political forces working as they do have enabled a leveling process to take place.

As these lines are written the words of Socrates, expressed over two thousand years ago, come to mind — "until political greatness and wisdom meet in one, cities will never have the rest from their evils, no, nor the human race."

Finally, to insure effective city government it will require the making of the councilman's job more attractive and the encouraging of honest and capable citizens in the community to share in the responsibilities of self-government. Not only must able individuals be recruited for service, but they must be encouraged to remain in service long enough so that the community will receive a maximum return from its investment in them. Too many business and social leaders refrain from openly mingling in the rough-and-tumble of local politics. Private welfare and philanthropy offer in their minds a more respectable way of performing one's civic duties. The danger of receiving a severe jar to one's ego is far less hazardous than it is for one seeking an elective public office.

VII

Austin's City Managers

AUSTIN HAS HAD ONLY SEVEN CITY MANAG-
ers since adopting the council-manager form of government
over forty-six years ago.

Although this would average about eight years' service
each, one manager served seventeen years, another twelve
years, and two have served less than three years. The more
recent box score has indicated that troublesome times have
had marked effect on tenure for city managers in Austin.
At this writing, the city council has employed Austin's
seventh city manager.

The new public administration's humanistic approach
places the city manager on the front lines of every urban
change. Whether or not he can successfully play the role
of an aggressive policy advocate, as some would have him
do, is another matter. Be it remembered that he holds his
position at the will of the council, the elected representatives
of the community. The city belongs to the elected repre-

76

sentatives, not the manager. To compete with the council as a spokesman for the public places him in a most dangerous position. Experience proves that in the long run, when there is a contest between the council and the manager, it is the manager who comes out second best. A study of Austin's city managers clearly demonstrates this truth.

A city manager may propose action he thinks the council should consider. As a full-time executive responsible to the council, he provides advice, suggestions and data which give the council a basis for decision. This is his obligation, and in so doing, he is not usurping the logical domain of the elected official.

The city manager is the chief administrator of his city. While the council finally determines the policy, the manager may, and should, play an important role in the process of policy making. He is surrounded with the tools, such as research, planning, department heads, experience and others; because of these he is well equipped to visualize the broad and overall objectives of various city programs. He is not only interested in trying to develop these programs, but he lends his support to those his government is sponsoring.

The city manager and his staff are active in public relations. Once the council has acted, he, the mayor, and the council assume the responsibility for selling the policy to the people and for developing approval through public education. This does not detract from the council's political leadership.

Over the years, the role of the city manager has not been static. During the early years of council-manager government it was generally believed that there was a sharp line of demarcation between legislation and administration. In fact, this was never true. Policy making and administration do not come in separate compartments. There is an overlapping between the two which requires teamwork both in policy making and in its execution through the administrative process. For council-manager government to function well the council and the manager must be on the same team, and there must be a mutual respect for the other's honesty and integrity.

It is impossible to describe any manager as a "typical" manager or any council as a "typical" council — they vary as to personality, time, place and conditions under which they operate. Councils tend to seek trained managers today. The job calls for "generalists" — men able to oversee a wide range of administrative operations — rather than "specialists." There are good managers who have engineering, public relations, or financial backgrounds, who develop a broad view of public management.

C. H. Garland's statement is well taken. To quote, "The skill of the administrator is only partly capable of universal acquisition. The final and highest expression of it, like the expression of all art, is personal. Judgment, force of character, and tact . . . cannot be measured. They are estimated by more subtle means; they must be gauged by personal reactions which cannot be expressed statistically . . . and if administration is to arise above mediocrity, room must always be left for the full play and exercise of those personal qualities which distinguish creative art from scientific formulae."[1]

A brief profile of Austin's city managers follows:

Adam R. Johnson, Jr.

Place of Birth — Burnet County, Texas
Education — Secondary School
Career Pattern — Worked in and later managed a lumberyard, Marble Falls, Texas; member of Burnet County Draft Board, 1918; served in World War I; cotton buyer in Austin, 1920; President, T. H. Williams and Company, 1922-1924; Manager of the Adam

---

[1] C. H. Garland, *Public Management*, February, 1932.

Johnson Company (Department Store, Austin), 1924-1926; City Manager, Austin, July 28, 1926-June 1, 1933, when he resigned

Age When Becoming Manager of Austin —54

Adam R. Johnson was Austin's first city manager and the imprint which he left upon the city's administrative machine exists until this day. He served from July 28, 1926 until June 1, 1933, when a long-developing opposition group won a council majority. He resigned as a matter of course.

Throughout his seven years in office he administered the city as the charter provided. Many seemed to believe that the council followed his dictates, and that he ran the city with an iron hand. Perhaps it would be more accurate to say, as Walter E. Long, Sr., who was secretary of the Austin Chamber of Commerce at the time, did, "Adam Johnson led his council." He was the son of a Confederate Brigadier General, had been an officer in the army during World War I, and no doubt his training and experience contributed to his direct and forthright speech and actions. He was honest and fearless — one who possessed a burning desire to build an efficient city administration. When he became the city's chief administrator, patronage ended and the law was enforced equally upon all, be they friend or foe. He not only believed in an efficiently run government, but he was equally insistent upon the city providing the needed services to the community. He demonstrated concern in the human side of government as well as the physical.[2] It was he who set up Austin's first recreation department and built a dam which created Barton Springs Swimming Pool.

Adam Johnson was not nonpartisan. He identified himself with the citizens' group that had established council-manager government in Austin and he never forsook them. He was president of the Chamber of Commerce at the time the Chamber took an active part in the campaign for man-

---

2 See Adam R. Johnson, *A Brief History of Austin's City Government Since the Inauguration of Council-Manager Form of Government,* Austin, 1932, Privately reproduced.

ager government. From the very beginning the groups that formed the political opposition came to regard the city manager as their chief opponent. He became the principal issue in the elections of 1927, 1931, and 1933.

The council did not run interference for the manager. They did not undertake the functions of explaining the work of the administration to the public. While the manager apparently did an excellent job of running the administration, the council failed to maintain public support. The Johnson administration was not close to the people. They regarded the manager as the city government.

Adam Johnson was a native Texan who grew up more interested in hunting and fishing than in attending school. He became a merchant, a builder, a soldier, and above all, an administrator. He attracted good men — he was by nature a managing man.

Three days after he became city manager the headlines in the local paper ran — "Axe wielded at City Hall; Four positions abolished by manager."

Guiton Morgan

Place of Birth — Dallas, Texas

Education — B.S. degree in Civil Engineering, The University of Texas

Career Pattern — MKT Railroad, field and drafting work, 1920; Texas State Highway Department, Bridge Division, Bridge Designer, 1921-1922; Texas State Highway Department, Resident Engineer, Bridge Construction, 1922-1923; Texas State Highway Department, Assistant Bridge Engineer, Bridge and Road Design Construction, 1923-1931; Travis County, County Engineer, 1931-1933; City Manager, Austin, 1933-1950

Professional and Honorary Organizations —

American Society for Professional Engineers

American Society for Military Engineers
International City Management Association
Texas City Managers Association
Reserve Officers Association
Age When Becoming Manager of Austin — 36

Mr. Guiton Morgan's appointment as the second city manager of Austin came as a complete surprise to many. It had been rumored that the council would choose someone who had been active in the campaign and who would see that the workers for the party were properly rewarded. This did not happen. With the coming of the Miller-Morgan administration both the theory and practice of council-manager relations were changed from that of the McFadden-Johnson; however the personnel at city hall remained largely intact. Adam Johnson left the city with a good administrative staff.

Mr. Morgan brought to the manager's office a completely different personality from that possessed by the former manager. He held a degree in engineering from The University of Texas, had held technical administrative positions at both the state and county levels of government and been in private employment for a short while before assuming the city manager's position.

Mr. Morgan has a pleasing personality, but not a dominating one. He was excellent in working with his council and with the public. At no time did he seek to make headlines or go out of his way to court the news media. He worked behind the scenes. There was no hesitancy on his part to present the facts to the council and he would state his point of view. This, however, was done in private meetings with the council or in executive sessions. Guiton Morgan was never one to attempt to handle a hot poker on the front porch. He was inconspicuous politically and never took an active part in local politics. There was never a desire on his part to seek credit or glory. This he was willing to leave for the mayor and council.

The Miller-Morgan team was a very successful one.

81

On many, many occasions Mayor Miller would say, "The people elect us to office, not the manager. We must run the government because we are responsible to them." The manager accepted this concept of council-manager relations. He believed that the council was the source of his authority. "I have the same relation to the council that one of my department heads has to me. It is the source of all of my authority," he would say.[3] He regarded his authority as being delegated by the council. Morgan's influence over the policy making of the council was accomplished through the use of administrative and personal methods rather than through the exercise of his legal rights. He always provided the council with detailed recommendations and supporting data, on both administrative and policy matters — if they prevailed, it was because of the weight of expert evidence rather than the result of strong personal leadership.

The manager regarded it his job to keep his council informed as to what went on at city hall. He believed it part of his responsibility to make the council "look good." The council ran interference for him; he was protected from the attacks of political enemies that Adam Johnson suffered, and which finally led to the defeat of the McFadden-Johnson administration in 1933.

Guiton Morgan served Austin a total of seventeen years. Of this total he was on leave for approximately three and one-half years serving in the armed services. This is by far the longest term of service for an Austin manager. He was only thirty-six years of age when he accepted the position — the youngest in Austin's history. Leaving city hall to go into private business in Austin was of his own choosing.

---

3 This writer served as a councilman during Mr. Morgan's last years at city hall.

Walter E. Seaholm

Place of Birth — Austin, Texas

Education — B.S. degree in Electrical Engineering, 1920, The University of Texas

Career Pattern — Employed by T.P.&L. during the summers while in the university; Electrical Engineer, Stone and Webster, 1919-1922; City of Austin, Electrician, 1922-1926; Superintendent, Electric Department, 1926-1933; Electrical Department, Director of Utilities, 1934-1942; Acting City Manager, 1942-1945; Electrical Department, Director of Utilities, 1945-1950; City Manager, 1950-1955

Professional and Honorary Organizations —

Tau Beta Pi

President, Ex-Student Association, The University of Texas, 1939

American Institute of Electrical Engineers

President, Travis Chapter, Texas Society of Professional Engineers, 1939

President, National Society of Professional Engineers, 1940

President, Austin Kiwanis Club, 1939

Honorary Degree of Knight Commander of Court of Honor of the 32nd Degree (KCCH)

Potentate, Ben Hur Shrine

Vice-President, International City Management Association, 1953

President, Texas City Managers Association, 1955

Age When Becoming Manager of Austin — 53

Walter E. Seaholm loved his hometown. He was Austin born and educated and it was here that he practically spent his entire life. More than any other manager in Austin's history he was more a part of her social and governmental fabric. He devoted his life to making this city a better place to live — he was dedicated to the service of his fellowman.

Even in his younger years, Walter Seaholm was a man

83

of great courage and firm conviction. It was during the late 1920s that the Texas Power and Light Company attempted to buy Austin's electrical system. This they would have done had it not been for young Seaholm, who at the time was in charge of the city's electrical department. When Texas Power and Light, after a check by their own engineers, found that the cost per unit of the electrical energy produced by the Austin plant was cheaper than they could produce it, they called off their testing engineers and gave up their efforts to buy the Austin system.

Since 1926 the electrical department has transferred from their gross revenues over ninety million dollars to the city's general fund.

Mr. Seaholm's appointment to the manager's position was a popular selection.[4] He was liked and respected both inside and outside city hall. The employees regarded him as a friend and the citizens looked upon him as a community leader. By nature he was careful, cautious, and analytical — not quick to make a decision. On the other hand, when once he reached a decision, based upon what he believed to be the facts, he was not quick to change his belief. He found it difficult to compromise. At times he seemed to hold to the theory that many city problems disappear if only given time. It is true that the passage of time solves some issues, but it also magnifies others.

Austin, during the early fifties, was beginning to show more growing pains, the character of the community was undergoing change, all of which reflected in the type of individual elected to the city council. The philosophy of government was being modified, less emphasis was placed on the physical side of city government — citizens and groups were beginning to become more involved in city programs. These and other facts had their effects upon

---

4 The author was a member of the council at the time of Mr. Seaholm's appointment as city manager.

council-manager relationships, with the result that they parted ways on February 9, 1955.

The city's political leadership was not located at city hall during this particular period. The press appeared to be primarily interested in selling its wares.

Austin owes much to Walter E. Seaholm. It was men like he, and many others who worked with him, in light, water, sewage, and public works departments that provided services for which the city may justly be proud today.

William T. Williams, Jr.

Place of Birth — Angleton, Texas

Education — Undergraduate, The University of Texas, 1924-1926; University Afloat, 1926-1927; LL.B. degree, The University of Texas, 1930

Military Service — Active duty as Army Reserve Officer, 1942-1946; in Active Army Reserve, 1946-1968; retired as Colonel, 1968

Career Pattern — Private practice of law, 1930-1940; Assistant City Attorney, Austin, 1940-1942; Assistant City Attorney, 1946-1947; City Tax Assessor and Collector, 1947-1949; Assistant City Attorney, 1949-1951; City Attorney, 1951-1955; City Manager, Austin, 1955-1967

Professional and Honorary Organizations —

Retired Officers' Association

Reserve Officers' Association, former President — Austin Chapter

Delta Theta Phi

State Bar of Texas

Travis County Bar Association

American Judicature Society

International City Management Association

Who's Who in America since 1968

Age When Becoming Manager of Austin — 47

William T. Williams, Jr. served Austin a total of twenty-three years — twelve of these as her manager. For nine years he was either assistant or City Attorney, and the two additional years he served as City Tax Assessor and Collector, thus he came to the manager's office with a good understanding of the city's activities and her personnel. With the exception of the time he spent on active duty with the military, most of his years since early youth had been spent in Austin. He was well acquainted with Austin and her people. Mr. Williams became the city's fourth manager in a period of twenty-nine years — all of them local men.

Mr. Williams was a prodigious worker; he spent long days and most of his weekends at city hall. Working days of ten or twelve hours did not seem to trouble him — it apparently was his recreation. He was thorough and exacting of himself and others — his recommendations to the council were based upon data carefully collected, screened, and analyzed, much of which he did personally. Williams was never a "Yes Man" — all propositions were placed under scientific scrutiny and proof.

He spent hours in private sessions with department heads, city employees, and the council — city hall knew Bill Williams and she respected him. No doubt he carried far more than his share of the work load.

By no stretch of the imagination was he public relations minded in the ordinary sense of the word; nor was he politically activated. He was diligent, sincere, capable and honest — believing at all times that results should speak for themselves. At all times he was modest and unassuming. Politics and public relations, for the most part, he left to others.

Headlines in the local papers and television appearances were not a part of his makeup. He seemed more concerned in seeing that the job was well done than he did in having bouquets and honors cast in his direction.

Finally, after a number of differences arose between him

and some members of the council, he resigned to accept the position of Executive Vice-President, Walter Carrington Enterprises, located in Austin.

Robert M. Tinstman

Place of Birth — Johnstown, Pennsylvania

Education — B.S. degree in Architectural Engineering, Pennsylvania State University; M.A. degree, Governmental Administration, Wharton School of Finance, University of Pennsylvania

Military Service — U.S. Army, 1951-1954; Served in Korea

Career Pattern — Assistant City Manager, Kansas City, Missouri, 1954-1960; City Manager, Abilene, Texas, 1960-1963; City Manager, Oklahoma City, 1963-1967; City Manager, Austin, 1967-1969

Professional and Honorary Organizations —

Tau Beta Phi

Sigma Tau

Texas City Managers Association

International City Management Association, etc.

Age When Becoming Manager of Austin — 39

Robert M. Tinstman was Austin's first out-of-state and out-of-town manager. Before coming to Austin he had lived in Texas a period of three years, that being during the time he served as Abilene's city manager. In years, he was the third youngest to hold the office of manager in Austin's history and he remained in that position for the briefest period of any manager — two years.

Many believe that he was Austin's most politically minded manager. To substantiate this point of view, they would point to his administrative appointments, saying that they were selected on a political rather than a basis of merit. Others contended that he played favorites with the council — which, if true, will sooner or later give any manager real trouble.

Mr. Tinstman has an outgoing personality; he is well informed in his field, possesses ideas and has the facility for communicating them to others, both in the spoken and written word. As a matter of fact, he spent much of his office time dictating memoranda and letters. He was public relations minded and many hours were passed with representatives of the news media. They responded in kind — he got a good press, and was protected on occasions when, if the facts had been publicized, might have proven embarrassing to the city administration.

Tinstman, in his public relations activities reflected the mode of operations of the majority of the council under which he worked. They loved the limelight, the headlines, the pomp and ceremony, and the credit that controlled publicity provides. Given a different set of conditions he might well have remained the city's administrative head for a longer period and contributed significantly to the city's administrative organization.

In politics, as in horse racing, if you bet on the wrong horse, you lose.

Lynn H. Andrews

Place of Birth — Arcadia, Louisiana

Education — B.S. degree in Civil Engineering, Louisiana Polytechnic Institute

Career Pattern — Engineer for Soil Conservation Service, Louisiana, 1935-1941; Planner, Traffic Engineer, Administrative Coordinator for Mayor, Shreveport, Louisiana, 1941-1951; Assistant to City Manager, Lubbock, Texas, 1951-1955; Assistant City Manager, San Antonio, Texas, 1955-1958; City Manager, San Antonio, Texas, 1958-1961; City Manager, St. Petersburg, Florida, 1961-1969; City Manager, Austin, Texas, 1969-1972

Professional and Honorary Organizations —
"Government Figure" in San Antonio, 1958
"Outstanding Salesman" San Antonio Exchange Club, 1961
"Good Government Award," St. Petersburg Jaycees, 1963
"Top Management Award," St. Petersburg Sales and Marketing Executives, 1969
Past President of the Florida Managers' Association
Texas City Managers' Association
International City Management Association
Age When Becoming Manager of Austin — 55

Anyone assuming the position of city manager today is a glutton for punishment. This statement should be underscored for an individual undertaking the position in Austin in 1969. Austin, like many urban communities, for the last score or more years, had felt the effects of urbanization and industrialization. Austin was more than the home of educational institutions and the seat of state government. It was and is a rapidly growing, throbbing city, bursting at the seams. Economic, social and political conditions had greatly changed from what they had been in the forties and fifties.

Shortly after the council of 1967 took over at city hall the last of the series of Austin-trained managers departed. The new council told the citizens that a new era had arrived, and that municipal services long neglected would be improved, and new ones added. The record does not reflect that this came to pass. Conditions as they existed at the time are well expressed in the old Chinese proverb — "Big noise on the stairway — little comes down."

Although the full council of five members chosen in 1967 sought reelection in 1969, the mayor and two other members were defeated — the defeated ones had been the most vocal members of the group. The 1969 council — now seven in number — while a number of them were capable and dedicated to improving Austin's city government, they were unable to form or work as a team; they were independent actors on a stage that was new to some of them.

89

A majority of them were never loved by the local news media or the "kingmakers," either before or after their election.

By 1969 Austin's governmental structure had grown unwieldy. There was a lack of coordination between the various departments and agencies of city government. Each appeared to be operating somewhat as a separate and independent unit; thirty departments or agencies were reporting directly to the city manager. Austin needed an administrative reorganization of her city government.

The city had no real political leadership. Briefly these were some of the major factors which existed in Austin when Lynn H. Andrews became city manager on November 15, 1969.

Mr. Andrews has spent a greater part of his working and professional life in municipal administration. No previous Austin manager could top or equal his managerial experience at the time he took office. He was perhaps more action minded than any of those preceding him — save Adam Johnson. It was not his nature to administer a "caretaker government." Andrews was not public relations minded. This seems to be true of his actions both inside and outside city hall. He was honest, fair, quick spoken, and brutally frank. His personal and administrative characteristics were very similar to those of Austin's first manager — "a hard nosed administrator." Again, like Johnson, he believed in administering the city according to the city charter. Adam Johnson was shot while he held the office, and became a campaign issue in three city elections.

To make the manager's job more arduous, the council of 1971 gives the impression of following the policy of "on again, off again." What appears to be the most popular position at any given time is the one the council hastens to assume — it may be changed at next council meeting. Such actions make efficient administration impossible. Lynn H. Andrews, apparently being convinced that the city council with whom he worked, did not, in fact, want a city manager, resigned to take a position in private industry.

Dan H. Davidson

Place of Birth — Panhandle, Texas
Education — B.S. degree in Park Management, Texas Technological University
Career Pattern — U.S. Army in Europe, 1953-1955; Chief of Advance Planning, City Council Coordinator, San Antonio, Texas, 1959-1961; Assistant City Manager, St. Petersburg, Florida, 1961-1969; Deputy City Manager, Austin, Texas, 1969-1972; City Manager, Austin, Texas, 1972-
Professional and Honorary Organizations —
Jaycee "Most Outstanding Young Man Under 35," St. Petersburg, Florida, 1967
Kiwanis Club, "Layman of the Year Award," St. Petersburg, Florida, 1969
Texas City Managers' Association
International City Management Association
Age When Becoming Manager of Austin — 38

Dan H. Davidson's appointment as Austin's seventh city manager on August 31, 1972, after the passage of more than five months since Mr. Lynn H. Andrews resigned the position on March 8, came as no surprise to most Austin residents. Mr. Davidson came to Austin with Mr. Andrews as deputy city manager and served as acting manager from the former's departure until his own appointment as the city's chief administrative officer. Austin is Davidson's first effort in a top administrative post, having served in the second position both in St. Petersburg and in Austin. On the day he assumed his present position he stated, "I believe the council-manager form of government as it is originally

---

5 *The Austin American,* September 1, 1972.

91

conceived is for the mayor and councilmen to represent political aspects, while the administrative staff should worry about implementing policy."[5]

These words are being added to a manuscript which is now in galley proof, and at a time when Mr. Davidson's appointment to his new position is only one day old. It would be unfair and without the basis of fact for the author to say more than that Mr. Davidson's education and experience should qualify him for the position of city manager. He served well as deputy city manager.

As stated elsewhere in this narrative, both the theory and the practice of council-manager government have undergone change since the days of Staunton, in the Shenandoah Valley of Virginia, when the term "manager" was used in 1908. At that time the office of "general manager" was created by ordinance.

Most councils appear to function best with managers of their own choosing. At the risk of error, which is so common of any general statement, there is much evidence to show that mayors and councils today like to meddle in administration, whether it be Austin, Texas or many cities throughout the land who call themselves council-manager cities. The decision is made by the mayor and council in each case as to whether they want a manager or an errand boy in the manager's office. Many councilmen do not know what council-manager government is. Strong, capable managers do not make good errand boys — they do not need a job that badly.

Summary

No two cities are alike and no two managers are alike. A given city will need different types of managers at different times. Insofar as possible each should have a manager to fit its particular needs. A review of Austin's managers demonstrates that each suited the needs of the city at the

92

particular time of his appointment. As conditions changed he stayed for a while or passed on, depending upon the circumstances. However, this much is certain: They were all men of good character, capable, and professional in their approach towards the management of this city. They all made a contribution to Austin's betterment — some more, some less.

Every manager knows today that he must be a champion of projects and a good administrator, a policy maker and an implementer, council oriented and community oriented, a person always seeking efficiency, one capable of advocating change and of adapting to change. He is also quick to recall that Jesus was betrayed by one of his own disciples. The judge gave the people the choice between the prophet of love and peace and a robber. The mob, led by the so-called best people, preferred Barabbas and let Jesus go to be crucified.

Most councilmen have a short memory when the pressure is applied.

VIII

Epilogue
(The Author's Personal Remarks)

THESE ARE THE BEST TIMES AND THESE ARE
the worst times. We live amid unparalleled material prosperity. On the other hand, our urban centers are decaying.
Racial tensions exist and perhaps are building — all the
time the pollution of our environment continues. Most
citizens want more services, employees desire more money,
and everyone wants lower taxes. There are demands to subsidize the privately owned bus company or for the city
to go into the transportation business; the same is true of
the ambulance service. More funds are demanded for the
arts — like symphony orchestras, theatres, museums — requests for more playgrounds, tennis courts, golf courses
and swimming pools are eternal, and additional support
for mental health and mental retardation is endless; thus

94

it goes on and on. All the time cities are confronted with insufficient revenues to cope with these and other problems.

Austin's response in recent years to her problems is commonplace — namely, seeking a solution in Washington to her social ills. What the citizen really needs is more identity with his local government. People must see city hall as themselves.

The Problem of Competence

Modern urban conditions place new demands on citizenship. Public decisions are increasingly made on the basis of considerable research and technical advice. For the citizen this means that a patriotic determination to participate is hardly sufficient if he hopes to be effective in dealing with large organizations and complex and technical problems — pollution control, community health, library and city hall location, for example. Public pressure is no longer enough. That pressure must be sharply focused on the technical aspect of a problem. The information available to citizens is generally poor and poorly presented. Democratic development therefore involves more than merely making the opportunity for participation available through the usual channels. We need to fashion processes that permit translation of private skills, information needs and perceptions into effective public participation in order to make citizens more independent of bureaucratic spoon-feeding and more competent to deal with public issues and officials.

The time has come when the citizen needs to demand and support competency at city hall. One must respect and reward performance. It is not good enough to say that an individual tried awfully hard — the question is, did he do the job?

There are those who contend that a frequent turnover in the offices of city councilmen offers a splendid opportunity to bring new ideas to city problems. As a matter of fact, there seems to be little evidence to substantiate the statement. The councilman must learn his job in much the same manner of one who serves an apprenticeship or an internship prior to becoming a technician or practicing a profession. A frequent turnover among those who have begun to acquire this type of experience and expertise appears to result in decisions being made by novices only vaguely familiar with the consequences of their actions. Unfortunately in Austin this turnover has occurred too frequently in recent years and has denied the community the opportunity to make use of the skills and knowledge acquired by more experienced members of the council. The 1971-1973 council is perhaps the worst in this respect in Austin's history — with the exception of one member who served the term of 1967-1969, it is composed of entirely new members.

As one observes some councilmen in action there is a feeling, rightly or wrongly, that perhaps nature designed them for humbler jobs. On the other hand, if the late John F. Kennedy was correct when he said, "Politics is a jungle — torn between doing the right thing and staying in office," it is readily understandable why so few individuals of outstanding character and ability seek service on city councils. It could easily be that the public gets better individuals in these positions than it deserves.

One desiring to climb the political ladder is well advised not to start at the municipal level. Only one Austin councilman since 1900 has been successful in being elected to a state or a national office. As a matter of fact, few have sought higher political offices. If one does his job on the council, he receives many body blows and political scars. A councilman lives with the people he governs.

A councilman often feels a sense of political frustration. The city today is built around many poles. The leadership in the community is a coalition in so many cases. There is political leadership, economic and social leadership. Sometimes these are fused as in the case of Austin today where the political and economic are blended, neither of which is held by those in official positions at city hall. This rather complex situation makes an understanding on the part of the voter difficult.

To make it more so, he sees a lessening of city pride and an emphasizing of the neighborhoods on the one hand, and on the other, it appears that the national community is becoming increasingly more meaningful. At the same time various councils of governments are becoming more and more responsible for regional types of responsibilities, so they are likely sooner or later in effect to become regional governments. Are cities going to be forced to assume a secondary role in the solution of urban problems?

Do honest, capable, and sincere individuals desire to seek service on city council if they are shouldered with the responsibility, but are relieved of the decision-making process?

Here is a case in point. In 1970, the Austin city council instructed its city manager to make an audit of the management practices and procedures of Brackenridge Hospital. Among other things, it was found that approximately fifty cents of every city tax dollar was being spent at Brackenridge — that the hospital was being operated at a deficit of some $3,000,000 (1970-1971). Much of this loss was attributable to welfare. In other cases one might point to poor management. For instance, Brackenridge East was serving only four or five patients at a cost of over $250,000 per year to the City of Austin before it was closed. The contract with the pathologists assured them exorbitant pay — the senior one receiving a monthly check from the city in excess of $6,500 for his personal services — in addition he had the privilege of running a laboratory on the side, which he did. A nursing school which had existed for years and known only as a diploma or trade school, was found to be badly in need of the supervision of professional educators.

Its discontinuance had been recommended by the City-County Affairs Committee Concerning Health in early 1970. The Texas Nurses Association made a similar recommendation, suggesting that it be placed under some educa-

97

tional institution, and the faculty of the Brackenridge School of Nursing itself, in 1968, voted it be discontinued. In addition, the school had been poorly administered for a number of years — tuition was paid for its students who took courses at The University of Texas in Austin, their textbooks were provided, taxi fares paid for their transportation to and from the university, and bands or orchestras hired at times for some of their parties — all of this at taxpayers' expense.

Over the protests of the medical staff of Brackenridge Hospital, the opposition of a few nurses employed on the staff of the Nursing School, the outcries of some of the school alumni, and the pleading of a sprinkling of Austin's doctors, the majority of the members of the Austin city council instructed the city manager to negotiate a contract with proper authorities at Southwest Texas State University to supervise and operate, in cooperation with Brackenridge Hospital, a school of nursing. This was done, but before the agreement was signed, the university authorities suddenly informed the city manager that the university's Board of Regents had decided to postpone any action until after the Austin city council election in 1971. The master's voice was heard and heeded. The final decision was taken out of the hands of the council in 1970.

If similar therapy were applied to the saga of Austin's buses in 1970 or to the increase in gas rates, one would again reach some of the roots of the city's well-established power structure.

Some Basic Changes

Some basic changes are taking place in government today and with the people who support it. Suddenly cheating and stealing is not known as such, if it takes place in government. Then, it is just politics. Wheeling, dealing and scheming has become rather commonplace — maybe it was always thus.

Austin has never had a scandal of major proportions occur wherein a member of its official family was involved. City officials have been exceptionally free of such transgressions. In 1968, land originally owned by the City of Austin and formerly the site of a Federal Fish Hatchery on the shores of Town Lake was declared surplus by the Department of the Interior and transferred to the Department of Health, Education and Welfare, only a short time before Pres. Lyndon Johnson left the White House. Apparently, over the objections of some H.E.W. officials, a non-profit corporation was formed with Frank C. Erwin, then Chairman of The University of Texas Board of Regents; Roy Butler, then President of the Austin School Board and now mayor of the City of Austin; and others, in the name of the Austin Geriatrics Center, Inc. and was brought into existence. The name of the center has since been changed to the Rebekah Baines Johnson Center in honor of the former President's mother. It is reported that transaction was not finally settled until after Mr. Johnson contacted Pres. Richard Nixon regarding the matter. At the time of the negotiations, no city official was personally involved. While the terms of the act of incorporation are not easily understood, the city has never raised the question of legality.

Every generation makes mistakes, always has and always will. The greatest mistake of the present generation is the abdication of its responsibility to youth and the various minority groups. When was this country ever ruled by such contingencies? Since when have the young and immature ruled this country? By virtue of what right, utterly without the benefit of learning, experience, judgment, wisdom or responsibility do they become the sages of our time? These people did not invent sensitivity; they do not own it; and what they seek to attain all mankind has sought to achieve throughout the ages. Are we to approve the presumed attainment of it through drugs and permissiveness?

Over the years city administrations come and go. It seems to be a common failing with most of them to attempt to lead the public into believing that little was done at city hall until they appeared on the scene, or that their mistakes, faults, and blunders are the result of the previous council. In most cases nothing could be further from the truth. Only a weak council and an ineffective mayor attempt to alibi in such a manner. Instead of meeting the city's problems they spend most of their time appointing committees, studying problems, making loud noises about what they are going to do — if some action is finally taken it is altered or reversed soon afterwards depending upon the intensity of the pressure that is brought upon the council.

In a period of approximately forty-six years that council-manager government has been in existence in Austin, beginning with the McFadden-Johnson administration and extending through the Butler-Andrews administration, Austin has witnessed a great change in its approach to city administration. During the McFadden-Johnson period the council and manager worked as a team; they thought alike and acted quickly to meet what they believed to be the city's needs. City policy was a result of the council and the manager cooperative action. Administration was left entirely in the hands of the city manager. The council was composed of some of Austin's best-known businessmen who conducted the city's affairs as they would a corporate business.

Viewing the Butler-Andrews administration one might well question if the city was being operated under the same form of government as before. The council and the manager were not on the same team — apparently, there was little pulling together between the two; the council had provided itself with administrative assistants reporting directly to themselves at a total annual cost to the taxpayers of approximately seventy to seventy-five thousand dollars; the mayor and the council repeatedly told the public that they were running the city — not the manager.

100

There was no administrative detail too minor for the council to become involved in. The only thing constant at city hall today is change. Under such conditions administration comes to a halt, able administrative talent resigns, and morale at city hall reaches another low.

Without a doubt Austin has a new image. When the present mayor says certain laws are not being enforced because they are unpopular, one wonders where that leadership and backbone he spoke of before taking office in the spring of 1971 has gone. Apparently, if enough people endorsed burglary, the statutes against it would be disregarded. As it is, the dogs run free all over the city; cars and trucks double park in the business sections of Austin at peak periods of traffic congestion; and the so-called "street vendors" hawk their wares all over the city — all these things go unmolested in Austin today.

City Hall and the Press

In a democracy, there probably will always be a conflict between government and the press. This is good. On the other hand, misleading headlines, incomplete facts, bias, and brief statements will not long suffice in today's society. Truth, candor, and facts should prevail and be represented by all parties concerned. Credibility is not a one-way street — it is a problem for both the press and government.

Someone has said, "Fully informed citizen participation is the key to good government." No doubt much of the militant and the negative participation we have witnessed in recent years is based on insufficient or incorrect information, for which the news media is at least partially to blame. How to educate the people of the community to a satisfactory degree of knowledge and understanding of the city's problems without being changed with a Madison Avenue type of approach to the administration at city hall is still the unanswered question.

101

There are few city officials who could not improve their press relations. No doubt most reporters can be trusted to get things right as long as those responsible give them the facts. Unfortunately the reporter, unless he is an old-timer at city hall, knows little about municipal problems, or at least not their technical side, unless he is properly informed. By and large he is an outsider, he is not a specialist in city problems and their solutions, and his business is to report the news. An old-time reporter can be the best senior member on the council.

Austin has not had a seasoned and experienced reporter for any length of time on the city hall beat since the days of William J. Weeg for the local paper and Paul Bolton for KTBC-TV. Wray Weddell covered city hall for a few years after Weeg's departure and later the Travis County Court House for a period. In both cases the reporting was rather superficial. He later hit his stride when he was assigned to write a gossip column for the *Austin-Statesman*. This was continued until he left the paper in 1970.

In recent years, Austin city hall reporters, for the most part, have been new and inexperienced, fresh from college, and in some cases new in the community. Too many of those who demonstrated talent or ability soon departed for greener fields. They did not remain long enough to do some in-depth reporting which is so essential to a community's well-being. How can a fledgling in the field do a job? He must know implications, as well as background in depth on so many items which come under discussion at city hall.

We hear much about the freedom of the press today. Probably there is no such thing. It is controlled by the government in communist countries and in the capitalist countries by money. The latter, even at its worst, is preferable to the kind of a press which exists under government control. In any event, if freedom is to mean anything, it implies the right of the people to know the truth, not opinion disguised as fact.

The late G. B. Dealey, the famous publisher of the

Dallas Morning News, once said, "Every city will reach a place sooner or later where it ought to quit growing bigger and start growing better." This is much easier if that city has a great press. This means, among other things, an impartial press and one with the intestinal fortitude to "tell it as it is."

There was a time when we said that the news media followed the policy of "printing the news and raising hell." Today, the media seems more concerned in being a political participant than in being an objective observer and reporter. It too often seeks to be thought of as playing the role of the "king maker." To illustrate, take time to read the Austin local papers or listen to some of the radio and TV stations on a city election year.

Our Austin news media is no different from those of many other communities all over the land in its attempt to build up their favorite personalities, concentrating on the superficial civic "side-shows" at any given moment, and reciting in a mechanical fashion the daily happenings at city hall. Nor is Austin media different from others in resenting and retaliating when criticism is directed its way. The "watchdog" always resents being watched. As a matter of fact, it is very probable that city hall is more willing to accept censor than are the publishers and broadcasters.

As a member of the 1969-1971 Austin city council, I suggested on a number of occasions the need of the then administration moving to the use of more direct personal methods of communicating with the electorate and not relying entirely on the established news media. This is now happening in some cases at national, state, and local levels of government today.

It is too seldom recognized that both the city hall and the press are owned by the people and that there is common ground as well as battleground between them. Both must encourage qualified professional city journalists as the middlemen between the people and city hall. These men must be placed in positions of prestige and retained. Poor newsmen only widen the gap between the governed and the government. What is true of newsmen is equally true of city policy makers and city administrators. No city long remains a great city, once it falls under the control of errand boys, gadflies and publicity seekers.

The news media constitute a very important force in the achievement and the preservation of good government. They are the major and often the only source of day-to-day information about what happens at city hall.

Leadership

The mayor's office is perceptible, it is impressive and it is often taken for granted that its holder has the power and the capacity to act vigorously in the solution of the city's problems. How well he fulfills such expectations depends on both the man and the governmental structure under which he operates. Under the commission and the council-manager forms, the mayor is not legally the city's chief administrative officer. However, in both these forms the council and the community look to the mayor for leadership. No other member of the council is in so prominent a position to supply it, and as a matter of fact, it is seldom that a council will accept leadership from anyone other than the mayor.

Austin, over most of her history, has been fortunate in having strong leaders in the mayor's office. In recent years leadership has undergone a change. In both the 1967-1969 and the 1971-1973 councils, a strong council member has tended to dominate action at city hall, while the real power, for the most part, rests in the hands of those not holding public office. The 1969-1971 council was not controlled; it floundered at times because of the lack of leadership and the unwillingness on the part of its members to operate as a team.

Austin today is being built around several poles. As

the number of urban interests multiplies, so do the focuses of leadership. Local leadership is becoming more difficult. In fact, one might well ask the question: Is there anyone or group in Austin who is in such a position today — or can there be?

For a number of years Austin has lacked in political leadership at the top echelon of businessmen. Politics is the science of government and government today is our biggest business. The modern community lives by politics. Can a city compete in the urban world today without knowledge-able and articulate experts who are selfish to the extent that they fight for their city?

Let us close with the words of Socrates, "Until political greatness and wisdom meet in one, cities will never have rest from their evils, no, nor the human race."

Appendix A

Mayors and Councilmen of the City of Austin 1840-1973

The data for the period 1840 to 1850 is not available in the council minutes. The material used here comes from the following source:

> Works Project Administration
> District 9 W.P. 16206
> C.P. 165-1-66-109
> Texas Writers' Project
> Austin Copy (on file in the
> Austin-Travis County Collection
> of the Austin Public Library)

1840

Mayor: Edwin Waller (elected January 1840)
T. W. Ward (elected August 19, 1840)

ALDERMEN

Moses Johnson
J. W. Garrety
Wm. W. Thompson
Samuel Whiting

A. Savary
Nicholas McArthur
Jacob M. Harrell
C. Schoolfield

1841

Mayor: Moses Johnson

ALDERMEN

Jacob M. Harrell
Nicholas McArthur
A. Savary
G. K. Teulon

A. Beatty
H. B. Hill
Wm. W. Thompson
Beck (no initials available)

1842

Mayor: Asa Brigham
No record of Aldermen

1843

Mayor: Asa Brigham served only part of this year.
He was succeeded by J. W. Robertson.
No record of Aldermen

1844

Mayor: Joseph W. Robertson
No record of Aldermen

1845

Mayor: James M. Long
No record of Aldermen

<h1 style="text-align:center">1846</h1>

Mayor: James M. Long

<h2 style="text-align:center">ALDERMEN</h2>

J. M. Harrell	W. W. Thompson
Francis Dieterich	Dennis Walsh
James Cole	James G. Swisher

<h1 style="text-align:center">1847</h1>

Mayor: Jacob M. Harrell
No record of Aldermen

<h1 style="text-align:center">1848-1849</h1>

No records

<h1 style="text-align:center">1850</h1>

Mayor: S. G. Haynie

<h2 style="text-align:center">ALDERMEN</h2>

J. L. Holliday	J. M. W. Hall
A. H. Cook	Ben F. Johnson
James Cole	John E. Elgin

The data for the period 1851 to 1863 is taken from the Austin City Directory 1877-1878.

<h1 style="text-align:center">1851</h1>

Mayor: S. G. Haynie

<h2 style="text-align:center">ALDERMEN</h2>

J. M. W. Hall	John M. Swisher
James Holliday	James Cole
Charles Mann	T. Bostick

1852

Mayor: George J. Durham

ALDERMEN

James Cole	Harvey Smith
A. H. Cook	J. M. W. Hall
J. W. Blue	E. S. C. Robertson

1853

Mayor: Thomas W. Ward to September 1, 1853 followed by W. P. DeNormandie to December 31

ALDERMEN

H. Sublett	J. Haynie
J. M. W. Hall	Thomas Glascock
A. H. Cook	B. Grumbles

1854

Mayor: John S. Ford

ALDERMEN

E. H. Darter	L. D. Carrington
N. C. Raymond	G. H. Gray
T. Bostick	J. W. Lawrence

1855

Mayor: J. T. Cleveland

ALDERMEN

J. R. Jackson	M. A. Taylor
W. H. Carr	R. N. Lane
J. Harrell	O. Wilcox

110

1856

Mayor: E. R. Peck

ALDERMEN

James R. Jackson
John Bremond
George H. Gray

M. A. Taylor
George L. Walton
A. J. Lott

1857

Mayor: Thomas E. Sneed

ALDERMEN

Ben Bennett
John Bremond
Joseph Harrell
M. Ziller

Wm. M. Fowler
D. C. Freeman
B. F. Carter
P. DeCordova

1858

Mayor: B. F. Carter

ALDERMEN

W. A. Hamilton
H. H. Haynie
Thomas E. Sneed
E. Raven

W. A. Morris
James W. Smith
F. T. Duffau
P. DeCordova

1859

Mayor: B. F. Carter

ALDERMEN

J. H. Herndon
J. M. W. Hall
C. F. Millett
E. Raven

P. Priestly
F. T. Duffau
Abner Lee
N. G. Shelley

111

1860

Mayor: James W. Smith

ALDERMEN

J. T. Alexander

S. G. Haynie

J. H. Robinson

E. Raven

Wm. Hamilton

A. N. Hopkins

F. T. Duffau

T. D. Ormsby

1861

Mayor: James W. Smith

ALDERMEN

Ed Finnin

J. H. Robinson

W. H. Sharp

A. Eanes

Ben Henricks

F. T. Duffau

S. W. Goodrich

J. B. Costa

1862

Mayor: James W. Smith

ALDERMEN

J. H. Walker

J. H. Robinson

J. Harrell

W. H. Sharp

S. W. Goodrich

A. Eanes

Wm. Smyth

F. T. Duffau

The rest of the material for 1863 to 1973 was compiled from the City Council Minutes on file in the office of the City Clerk.

1863

Election of November 1862

Mayor: S. G. Haynie

112

ALDERMEN

Ward 1 — M. J. Walker (resigned January 19, 1863)
J. H. Herndon (elected January 30, 1863 to replace Walker)
Ward 2 — C. G. Keenan
Ward 3 — P. Priestly
Ward 4 — G. W. Glasscock
Ward 5 — W. A. Hamilton
Ward 6 — John Burlage
Ward 7 — W. Oliphant (resigned January 12, 1863)
W. H. Reynolds, elected to replace Oliphant February 14, 1863
Ward 8 — Wm. von Rosenberg

The council minutes for February 3, 1863 state that F. J. Roberts was elected to fill a position in Ward 7; however, at the April 1 council meeting all of the members were present and Roberts is not listed as a member.

1864

Election of November 1863

Mayor: S. G. Haynie

ALDERMEN

Ward 1 — J. A. Flack
Ward 2 — J. Bremond
Ward 3 — Robert Barr (resigned January 1864)
Swante Palm (elected January 1864 to replace Barr)
Ward 4 — George W. Glasscock
Ward 5 — W. A. Hamilton
Ward 6 — Eli Kirk
Ward 7 — W. H. Reynolds (resigned December 1863 before his 1864 term began)
J. R. McCall (elected January 1864 to replace Reynolds)
Ward 8 — W. Simpson

113

1865

(November 22, 1864 — October 1865)

Mayor: Thomas Ward

ALDERMEN

Ward 1 — B. O. Tong
Ward 2 — John Bremond, Sr. (resigned September 1865)
Ward 3 — Hugh Haralson (resigned October 12, 1865)
Ward 4 — George W. Glasscock (resigned September 1865)
Ward 5 — W. A. Hamilton
Ward 6 — John Holland (resigned August 7, 1865)
F. A. Foster (replaced Holland in August but resigned in October because of a feeling of ill will)
Ward 7 — J. R. McCall (resigned April 1865)
S. Spence (elected May 1, 1865 to replace McCall)
Ward 8 — S. W. Baker

October 1865 — February 1866

During the latter days of September and the month of October 1865 the following council was appointed by military authority.

Ward 1 — B. O. Tong
Ward 2 — J. M. W. Hall
Ward 3 — F. A. Foster (resigned on December 11, 1865)
Ward 4 — F. Brown
Ward 5 — John Hamilton (resigned December 5, 1865)
James Browne (appointed December 11, 1865 to replace Hamilton)
Ward 6 — John Holland
Ward 7 — S. Spence
Ward 8 — S. W. Baker

A. J. Hamilton, Provisionel Governor of Texas, called a general election to be held on February 8, 1866 in answer to a petition by the citizens of Austin.

Mayor: William Carr

ALDERMEN

Ward 1 — William von Rosenberg
Ward 2 — J. M. W. Hall
Ward 3 — Swante Palm
Ward 4 — Geo. W. Glasscock
Ward 5 — James Brown
Ward 6 — August Palm
Ward 7 — S. G. Haynie
Ward 8 — D. P. Kinney

1867

Election of November 1866

Mayor: William Carr

ALDERMEN

Ward 1 — William von Rosenberg
Ward 2 — J. M. W. Hall (died January 1867)
        J. H. Robinson (replaced Hall on April 11, 1867)
Ward 3 — Swante Palm
Ward 4 — Geo. W. Glasscock
Ward 5 — J. W. England
Ward 6 — August Palm
Ward 7 — Wm. Oliphant (resigned October 17, 1867 but was not replaced)
Ward 8 — Leander Brown

November 1867 — February 1, 1871

On November 1, 1867, the old city council was deposed by military order. A new one was appointed by military.

Mayor: Leander Brown

ALDERMEN

(All ward information not available)

Ward 2 — D. W. C. Baker
Ward 3 — Swante Palm
Ward 4 — E. Raven
Ward 6 — C. Domschke
      L. B. Collins
      J. W. England (not mentioned in minutes after December 1869)
      C. W. Fox
      B. C. Bennett (appointed December 7, 1868 to bring the number of aldermen to 8)

February 1, 1871 — November 1872

On February 1, 1871, Governor Davis reorganized the council.

Mayor: John Glenn

ALDERMEN

(Ward information not available)

      Thomas Adams
      J. Bremond
      J. L. Buaas
      E. Eggleston (On October 20, Eggleston's name disappeared from the minutes and was not returned)

Henry Madison

S. Mussina

Dr. Mills (was appointed but he turned down the offer and did not serve)

J. H. Robinson (appointed later in February 1871)

In January 1872 the Governor again reorganized the council. Bremond and Adams had been replaced by E. Wheelock and William Bruggerhoff. By the time of the election in November 1872, council members were as follows:

J. L. Buaas
Henry Madison
S. Mussina
J. H. Robinson
E. Wheelock
Wm. Brueggerhoff
Henry Willis (appointed June 1872)
R. Bertram (appointed October 1872)

1873

The first general election since November 1867 was held in November 1872. Officers were installed on November 16, 1872.

Mayor: T. B. Wheeler

ALDERMEN

Ward 1 — T. E. Sneed
Ward 2 — E. Bremond
Ward 3 — Ed Christian (resigned May 1873)
      G. T. Boardman (elected May 5 to replace Christian)
Ward 4 — George Susmann

117

Ward 5 — A. Scholtz
Ward 6 — Wm. Brueggerhoff
Ward 7 — J. H. Robinson
Ward 8 — J. W. Hannig
Ward 9 — A. H. Longley (elected July 5, 1873 after the 9th ward had been designated)
Ward 10 — Scipio Thompson (elected July 5, 1873 after the 10th ward had been designated)

November 1874 — November 1875
(2-year terms begin)

Mayor: T. B. Wheeler

ALDERMEN

Ward 1 — H. M. Metz (resigned January 6, 1875)
O. H. Cullen (elected February 1875 to replace Metz)
Ward 2 — E. Bremond
Ward 3 — George T. Boardman
Ward 4 — Ed Christian
Ward 5 — F. Dohme
Ward 6 — S. H. Todd
Ward 7 — A. Scholtz (resigned December 23, 1874)
S. Piper (elected February 1875)
Ward 8 — Wm. Brueggerhoff
Ward 9 — John H. Robinson
Ward 10 — N. B. Mitchell

November 1875 — November 1877

Mayor: T. B. Wheeler (resigned May 7, 1877)
J. C. DeGress became Mayor June 19, 1877

ALDERMEN

Ward 1 — D. A. James
118

Ward 2 — E. Bremond
Ward 3 — A. H. Cook, Jr.
Ward 4 — M. A. Taylor
Ward 5 — F. W. Chandler (resigned April 13, 1877)
       Robert Ward (elected May 4, 1877)
Ward 6 — J. Larmour
Ward 7 — David Sheeks (resigned last of December 1876)
       Otto Rost (replaced Sheeks in January 1877 but
          resigned in May)
       D. B. Withers (replaced Rost on June 4, 1877)
Ward 8 — A. Deffenbaugh
Ward 9 — J. H. Robinson
Ward 10 — F. O. Goodale (resigned April 1877)
       Louis Maas (elected April 10, 1877 to replace
       Goodale)

November 5, 1877 - November 3, 1879

Election held November 5, 1877

Mayor: J. C. DeGress

ALDERMEN

Ward 1 — N. B. Metz
Ward 2 — Jeremiah Sheehan
Ward 3 — G. Crow
Ward 4 — W. A. H. Miller (resigned March 11, 1878)
       E. Raven (elected March 23, 1878 to replace
       Miller)
Ward 5 — T. J. Markley (resigned March 1878)
       V. E. Vaughn (elected March 23, 1878 to replace
       Markley)
Ward 6 — L. M. Crooker
Ward 7 — H. M. Strong
Ward 8 — C. F. Millett
Ward 9 — Radcliff Platt
Ward 10 — Joseph Nalle

Mayor: J. C. DeGress, L. M. Crooker (dates unavailable. Council Minutes missing from June 6, 1881 to November 1881)

ALDERMEN

Ward 1 — N. B. Metz
Ward 2 — Jeremiah Sheehan
Ward 3 — George T. Boardman
Ward 4 — J. Tobin
Ward 5 — J. Wahrenberger
Ward 6 — L. M. Crooker (resigned August 21, 1880)
          H. H. Duff (replaced Crooker on September 14, 1880)
Ward 7 — Reichmann (died January 1881)
          Ed Huppertz (elected January 15, 1881 to replace Reichmann)
Ward 8 — G. L. Robertson
Ward 9 — E. S. Coombs (resigned May 3, 1880)
          Radcliff Platt (elected May 8, 1880 to replace Coombs)
Ward 10 — Joseph Nalle

November 15, 1881 — December 8, 1883)

On November 15, the new council was installed.

Mayor: W. A. Saylor

ALDERMEN

Ward 1 — N. B. Metz
Ward 2 — H. B. Kinney
Ward 3 — A. H. Cook, Jr. (resigned October 2, 1882)
          J. W. Lawrence (elected November 7, 1882 to replace Cook)

Ward 4 — J. Schuber
Ward 5 — Wm. Brueggerhoff (died at the end of June, 1883)
        Henry Pfannkuche (elected July 1883 to replace
        Brueggerhoff but resigned in October 1883)
        Max Maas (elected November 5, 1883 to replace Pfannkuche)
Ward 6 — B. Radkey (resigned July 23, 1883)
        J. W. Driskill (elected August 4, 1883 to replace Radkey)
Ward 7 — Ed Huppertz
Ward 8 — H. W. Moeller (resigned August 3, 1883)
        Thomas E. Sneed (elected August 10, 1883 to replace Moeller)
Ward 9 — Radcliff Platt
Ward 10 — W. G. Wilson

1884

The election of December 8, 1883 inaugurated a new system of selecting council members. There were two members elected from each ward. They were to serve two-year terms but were to be staggered so that ten would be elected each year. In order to begin the system, of the twenty men elected on December 8, ten would serve a one-year term and ten would serve a two-year term. They drew lots among themselves to determine who would serve the short and long terms.

Mayor: W. A. Saylor (resigned May 28, 1884 to take effect June 1)
       J. W. Robertson (replaced Saylor on June 14, 1884)

Two-Year Terms	One-Year Terms
Ward 1 — J. P. Schneider	W. J. Sutor
Ward 2 — Louis Hancock	B. S. Pillow
Ward 3 — B. C. Wells	T. J. Campbell

Ward 4 — J. Schuber   R. B. Underhill
Ward 5 — J. W. Robertson   Max Maas
         (resigned June
         1883 to be mayor)
         (George Warren
         replaced Robert-
         son June 27, 1884)
Ward 6 — J. W. Driskill   L. M. Crooker
Ward 7 — Albert Carrington   J. M. Odell
Ward 8 — R. J. Hill   G. L. Robertson
Ward 9 — R. Platt   Wm. Ervin
Ward 10 — W. B. Brush   Wm. Brennen

1885

Election December 1, 1884

Mayor: J. W. Robertson (still serving part of a two-year term)

ALDERMEN

	New	Old
Ward 1 —	C. S. Metz	J. P. Schneider
Ward 2 —	B. S. Pillow	L. Hancock
Ward 3 —	T. J. Campbell	B. C. Wells
Ward 4 —	R. B. Underhill	J. Schuber
Ward 5 —	Max Maas	G. Warren
Ward 6 —	L. M. Crooker	J. W. Driskill
Ward 7 —	J. M. Odell	Albert Carrington
Ward 8 —	R. H. Holman	R. J. Hill
Ward 9 —	Wm. Ervin	R. Platt
Ward 10 —	Wm. Brennen	W. B. Brush

1886

Election held December 11, 1885

Mayor: J. W. Robertson

ALDERMEN

New	Old
Ward 1 — J. P. Schneider	C. S. Metz
Ward 2 — C. E. Anderson	B. S. Pillow
Ward 3 — G. A. Brush	T. J. Campbell
Ward 4 — J. Schuber	R. B. Underhill
	C. G. Caldwell (elected January 1886 to finish Underhill's term)
Ward 5 — G. Warren	M. Maas (resigned December 21, 1885)
	August Giesen (elected January 1886 to finish Maas' term)
Ward 6 — W. B. Wortham	L. M. Crooker
Ward 7 — Dennis Corwin (resigned April 15, 1886)	J. M. Odell
Wm. Wellmer (elected May 17, 1886 to finish Corwin's term)	
Ward 8 — J. C. DeGress	R. Holman
Ward 9 — J. Cummings	Wm. Ervin
Ward 10 — W. B. Walker	Wm. Brennen (resigned January 4, 1886)
	F. E. Jones (elected January 18, 1886 to fill Brennen's term)

1887

Election of December 6, 1886

Mayor: J. W. Robertson (still serving part of a two-year term)

ALDERMEN

	New	Old
Ward 1 —	C. S. Metz	J. P. Schneider
Ward 2 —	C. E. Fisher	C. E. Anderson
Ward 3 —	T. J. Campbell	G. A. Brush
Ward 4 —	C. G. Caldwell	J. Schuber
Ward 5 —	A. W. Townsend	G. O. Warren
Ward 6 —	J. W. Graham	W. B. Wortham
Ward 7 —	J. M. Odell	W. A. Wellmer
Ward 8 —	J. W. Phillips	J. C. DeGress (resigned April 4, 1887) W. A. Alexander (elected April 15, 1887 to fill vacancy left by DeGress)
Ward 9 —	R. Platt	J. Cummings
Ward 10 —	F. E. Jones	W. B. Walker

1888

Election held December 1887

Mayor: Joseph Nalle

ALDERMEN

	New	Old
Ward 1 —	J. P. Schneider	C. S. Metz
Ward 2 —	B. S. Pillow	C. E. Fisher
Ward 3 —	G. A. Brush (resigned so close to the next regular election that he was not replaced by a special election)	T. J. Campbell
Ward 4 —	D. M. Wilson	C. G. Caldwell

124

Ward 5 — H. A. Linn   A. W. Townsend
Ward 6 — W. B. Wortham   J. W. Graham
Ward 7 — G. P. Assman   J. M. Odell (resigned
                                 November 1888)
Ward 8 — J. C. DeGress   J. W. Phillips
Ward 9 — M. Boland   R. Platt
Ward 10 — E. P. Haigler   F. E. Jones

1889

Election held December 3, 1888

Mayor: Joseph Nalle (still serving part of a two-year term)

ALDERMEN

New	Old
Ward 1 — C. S. Metz	J. P. Schneider
Ward 2 — W. F. North	B. S. Pillow
Ward 3 — F. G. Morris (elected for a regular two-year term)	J. R. Lawrence (elected to finish Brush's term)
Ward 4 — W. Ziller	D. M. Wilson
Ward 5 — A. W. Townsend	H. A. Linn
Ward 6 — J. W. Graham	W. B. Wortham
Ward 7 — J. B. Nitschke	G. P. Assman
Ward 8 — A. H. Newton	J. C. DeGress
Ward 9 — R. Platt	M. Boland
Ward 10 — F. E. Jones	E. P. Haigler

1890

Election of December 2, 1889

Mayor: John McDonald

ALDERMEN

New	Old
Ward 1 — J. P. Schneider	C. S. Metz
Ward 2 — C. E. Anderson	W. F. North
Ward 3 — Fred Carleton	F. G. Morris
Ward 4 — J. Schuber	W. Ziller
Ward 5 — H. A. Linn	A. W. Townsend
Ward 6 — J. L. Hume	J. W. Graham
Ward 7 — G. P. Assman	J. B. Nitschke
Ward 8 — J. W. Phillips	A. H. Newton
Ward 9 — M. Boland (died August 1890) D. L. Winfield (elected September 9, 1890 to fill Boland's seat)	R. Platt
Ward 10 — J. A. Jackson	F. E. Jones

1891

Election of December 1890

Mayor: John McDonald (still serving part of a two-year term)

ALDERMEN

New	Old
Ward 1 — W. J. Sutor	J. P. Schneider
Ward 2 — W. F. North	C. E. Anderson
Ward 3 — F. G. Morris	F. Carleton
Ward 4 — W. Ziller	J. Schuber
Ward 5 — A. W. Townsend	H. A. Linn
Ward 6 — J. W. Graham	J. L. Hume
Ward 7 — J. B. Nitschke	G. P. Assman
Ward 8 — A. H. Newton	J. W. Phillips
Ward 9 — R. Platt	D. L. Wingfield
Ward 10 — W. A. Glass	J. A. Jackson

126

Ward 11 — Robert Weyerman (term to expire in December 1892)   H. J. Ketchum (term to expire in December 1891)

On June 1, 1890 the council added the eleventh ward.

1892

Election of December 1891

Mayor: John McDonald

ALDERMEN

New	Old
Ward 1 — J. P. Schneider	W. J. Sutor
Ward 2 — C. E. Anderson	W. F. North
Ward 3 — W. D. Shelley	F. G. Morris
Ward 4 — J. Schuber	W. Ziller
Ward 5 — H. A. Linn	A. W. Townsend
Ward 6 — J. L. Hume	J. W. Graham
Ward 7 — G. P. Assman	J. B. Nitschke
Ward 8 — J. H. Warmoth	A. H. Newton
Ward 9 — K. C. Miller	R. Platt
Ward 10 — J. A. Jackson	W. A. Glass
Ward 11 — H. J. Ketchum	R. Weyerman

1893

Election of December 1892

Mayor: John McDonald (still serving part of a two-year term)

ALDERMEN

New	Old
Ward 1 — P. W. Powell	J. P. Schneider
Ward 2 — W. F. North	C. E. Anderson

Ward 3 — F. Fischer   W. D. Shelley
Ward 4 — Thomas Taylor   J. Schuber
Ward 5 — A. W. Townsend   H. A. Linn
Ward 6 — C. P. Raymond   J. L. Hume
Ward 7 — J. B. Nitschke   G. P. Assman
Ward 8 — L. Hancock   J. H. Warmoth
Ward 9 — R. Platt   K. C. Miller
Ward 10 — W. A. Glass   J. A. Jackson
Ward 11 — N. A. Dawson   H. J. Ketchum

1894

Election of December 4, 1893

Mayor: John McDonald

ALDERMEN

New	Old
Ward 1 — J. P. Schneider	P. W. Powell
Ward 2 — C. E. Anderson	W. F. North
Ward 3 — W. D. Shelley	F. Fischer
Ward 4 — R. C. Roberdeau	T. F. Taylor
Ward 5 — H. A. Linn	A. W. Townsend
Ward 6 — J. L. Hume	C. P. Raymond
Ward 7 — G. P. Assman	J. B. Nitschke
Ward 8— J. H. Warmoth	L. Hancock
Ward 9 — P. J. Lawless	R. Platt
Ward 10 — J. A. Jackson	W. A. Glass
Ward 11 — W. C. Redd	N. A. Dawson

1895

Election of December 1894

Mayor: John McDonald (still serving part of a two-year term)

128

ALDERMEN

New	Old
Ward 1 — P. W. Powell	J. P. Schneider
Ward 2 — W. F. North	C. E. Anderson
Ward 3 — A. C. Goeth	W. D. Shelley
Ward 4 — F. Fischer	R. C. Roberdeau
Ward 5 — A. W. Townsend	H. A. Linn
Ward 6 — W. H. Tobin	J. L. Hume
Ward 7 — J. B. Nitschke	G. P. Assman
Ward 8 — H. L. Haynes	J. H. Warmoth
Ward 9 — R. Platt	P. J. Lawless
Ward 10 — W. A. Glass	J. A. Jackson (resigned September 2, 1895. Not replaced until the December election)
Ward 11 — L. H. Glascock	W. C. Redd

1896

Election of December 1895

Mayor: Louis Hancock

ALDERMEN

New	Old
Ward 1 — J. P. Schneider	P. W. Powell
Ward 2 — F. M. Beaty	W. F. North
Ward 3 — W. D. Shelley	A. C. Goeth
Ward 4 — R. C. Roberdeau	T. F. Taylor
Ward 5 — H. A. Linn	A. W. Townsend
Ward 6 — Joseph Stumpf	W. H. Tobin
Ward 7 — C. Q. Horton	J. B. Nitschke
Ward 8 — S. E. Rosengren	H. L. Haynes
Ward 9 — P. J. Lawless	R. Platt
Ward 10 — A. J. Zilker	W. A. Glass
Ward 11 — W. C. Redd	L. H. Glascock

1897

Election of December 1896

Mayor: Louis Hancock (still serving part of a two-year term)

ALDERMEN

New	Old
Ward 1 — P. W. Powell	J. P. Schneider
Ward 2 — F. M. Maddox	F. M. Beaty
Ward 3 — F. Fischer	W. D. Shelley
Ward 4 — T. F. Taylor	R. C. Roberdeau
Ward 5 — A. W. Townsend	H. A. Linn
Ward 6 — A. M. Belvin	Joseph Stumpf
Ward 7 — J. B. Nitschke	C. Q. Horton
Ward 8 — H. L. Haynes	S. E. Rosengren
Ward 9 — R. Platt	P. J. Lawless
Ward 10 — Joseph Kuhn	A. J. Zilker
Ward 11 — W. D. Miller	W. C. Redd

1898

Election of December 6, 1897

Mayor: John Dodd McCall

ALDERMEN

New	Old
Ward 1 — M. Morris	P. W. Powell
Ward 2 — F. M. Beaty	F. M. Maddox
Ward 3 — W. D. Shelley	F. Fischer
Ward 4 — R. C. Roberdeau (Resigned November 7, 1898)	T. F. Taylor
Ward 5 — L. M. Crooker	A. W. Townsend

130

Ward 6 — J. Stumpf	A. M. Belvin
Ward 7 — C. Q. Horton	J. B. Nitschke
Ward 8 — S. E. Rosengren	H. L. Haynes
Ward 9 — J. McLemore	R. Platt
Ward 10 — A. J. Zilker	J. Kuhn
Ward 11 — W. C. Redd	W. D. Miller

1899

Election of December 5, 1898

Mayor: John Dodd McCall (still serving part of a two-year term)

ALDERMEN

New	Old
Ward 1 — P. W. Powell	M. Morris
Ward 2 — F. M. Maddox	F. M. Beaty
Ward 3 — F. Fischer	W. D. Shelley
Ward 4 — M. E. Groos (to serve until December 1901)	R. C. Walker (to finish Roberdeau's term)
Ward 5 — J. Brady	L. M. Crooker
Ward 6 — A. M. Belvin	J. Stumpf
Ward 7 — J. B. Nitschke	C. Q. Horton
Ward 8 — H. L. Haynes	S. E. Rosengren
Ward 9 — A. Fehr	J. McLemore
Ward 10 — J. Kuhn	A. J. Zilker
Ward 11 — W. D. Miller	W. C. Redd

April 1899 - April 1901

A general election on April 3, 1899 amended the City Charter providing that there would be seven wards with one council member from each ward serving for a term of two years.

Mayor: John Dodd McCall

131

ALDERMEN

Ward 1 — H. C. Nolen
Ward 2 — Milton Morris (resigned August 6, 1900)
        J. P. Schneider (elected October 1900 to replace
        Morris)
Ward 3 — F. Fischer
Ward 4 — J. Stumpf
Ward 5 — W. B. Dunham
Ward 6 — P. D. Mortimer
Ward 7 — W. A. Glass

April 1901 - April 1903

Mayor: R. E. White

ALDERMEN

Ward 1 — R. Gibbs (resigned October 7, 1901. Was not
        replaced until 1903)
Ward 2 — J. P. Schneider
Ward 3 — W. D. Shelley
Ward 4 — J. Stumpf
Ward 5 — J. B. Nitschke
Ward 6 — J. M. Shumate
Ward 7 — T. M. Low

In May 1901, the council decided to elect an additional member for each ward.

Ward 1 — W. C. Redd
Ward 2 — F. M. Maddox
Ward 3 — L. M. Crooker
Ward 4 — G. T. Hume
Ward 5 — William Ulit
Ward 6 — P. D. Mortimer
Ward 7 — W. B. Davis

132

April 1903 - April 1905

With this election, two councilmen were chosen for each ward, one elected from the ward and then the other at large.

Mayor: R. E. White

ALDERMEN

Ward 1 — W. D. Miller (at large); W. C. Redd (ward)
Ward 2 — J. P. Schneider (at large); F. M. Maddox (ward)
Ward 3 — W. D. Shelley (at large); L. M. Crooker (ward)
Ward 4 — G. T. Hume (at large); J. J. Macken (ward)
Ward 5 — J. B. Nitschke (at large); William Ulit (ward)
Ward 6 — J. M. Shumate (at large); H. L. Haynes (ward)
Ward 7 — T. D. Smith (at large); C. W. Moore (ward)

April 1905 - April 1907

Election of April 3, 1905

Mayor: W. D. Shelley

ALDERMEN

Ward 1 — W. D. Miller (at large); W. C. Redd (ward)
Ward 2 — P. W. Powell (at large); A. E. Cuneo (ward)
Ward 3 — E. von Rosenberg (at large); L. M. Crooker (ward)
Ward 4 — C. J. Armstrong (at large); J. J. Macken (ward)
Ward 5 — Henry Petri (at large); C. J. Wilhelm (ward)
Ward 6 — J. M. Shumate (at large) resigned October 4, 1906;
F. A. Scott (elected by the council to replace Shumate same day); H. L. Haynes (ward)
Ward 7 — T. D. Smith (at large) resigned December 3, 1906;
Wm. Holze (elected by the council to replace Smith same day); C. W. Moore (ward)

April 1907 - March 1909

Election of April 1, 1907

Mayor: F. M. Maddox

133

ALDERMEN

Ward 1 — W. D. Miller (at large); W. C. Redd (ward)
Ward 2 — P. W. Powell (at large), resigned July 9, 1907; W. J. Sutor (elected at large to replace Powell on November 23, 1907); A. E. Cuneo (ward)
Ward 3 — T. D. Smith (at large); L. M. Crooker (ward)
Ward 4 — C. J. Armstrong (at large); J. M. Meredith (ward)
Ward 5 — Henry Petri (at large); C. J. Wilhelm (ward)
Ward 6 — F. A. Scott (at large); H. L. Haynes (ward)
Ward 7 — C. B. Moreland (at large); C. W. Moore (ward)

March 1909 - April 1911

The Commission form of government was inaugurated in April 1909.
Commissioners were elected at large for a two-year term.

Mayor: A. P. Wooldridge

COMMISSIONERS

Eugene C. Bartholomew, Mayor Pro Tem
David B. Gracy
James P. Hart
P. W. Powell

April 1911 - April 1913

Mayor: A. P. Wooldridge

COMMISSIONERS

Eugene C. Bartholomew, Mayor Pro Tem
James P. Hart
P. W. Powell
T. D. Lockridge (resigned November 16, 1911)
Harry Haynes (replaced Lockridge on November 16, 1911)

134

April 1913 - April 1915

Mayor: A. P. Wooldridge

COMMISSIONERS

E. C. Bartholomew, Mayor Pro Tem
W. B. Anthony
H. L. Haynes
P. W. Powell

April 1915 - April 1917

Mayor: A. P. Wooldridge

COMMISSIONERS

Eugene C. Bartholomew, Mayor Pro Tem
H. L. Haynes
P. W. Powell
W. B. Anthony

April 1917 - April 1919

Mayor: A. P. Wooldridge

COMMISSIONERS

Eugene C. Bartholomew, Mayor Pro Tem
W. B. Anthony
H. L. Haynes
P. W. Powell

April 1919 - April 1921

Mayor: W. D. Yett

COMMISSIONERS

Harry L. Haynes, Mayor Pro Tem
C. F. Alford

John S. Ward
J. W. Graham

April 1921 - May 1923

Mayor: W. D. Yett

COMMISSIONERS

H. L. Haynes, Mayor Pro Tem
J. D. Copeland
Walter L. Eyres
George P. Searight

May 1923 - July 1926

Mayor: W. D. Yett

COMMISSIONERS

H. L. Haynes, Mayor Pro Tem
C. N. Avery
H. W. Nolen
George P. Searight

July 1926 - May 1927

The form of government changed to that of Council-Manager. Mayor and council were elected at large for two-year terms.

Mayor: P. W. McFadden

COUNCILMEN

Robert Mueller, Mayor Pro Tem (died January 1927)
Ben Barker
E. L. Steck (replaced Mueller in February 1927)
V. H. Pannell
D. C. Reed

May 1927 - May 1929

Mayor: P. W. McFadden

COUNCILMEN

V. H. Pannell, Mayor Pro Tem
Leo Mueller
E. L. Steck
D. C. Reed

May 1929 - May 1931

Mayor: P. W. McFadden

COUNCILMEN

V. H. Pannell, Mayor Pro Tem
Leo Mueller
D. C. Reed
E. L. Steck

May 1931 - May 1933

Mayor: P. W. McFadden

COUNCILMEN

Leo Mueller, Mayor Pro Tem
Simon Gillis
E. L. Steck
C. F. Alford

May 1933 - May 1935

Mayor: Tom Miller

COUNCILMEN

Oswald G. Wolf, Mayor Pro Tem
C. F. Alford
C. M. Bartholomew
Simon Gillis

May 1935 - May 1937

Mayor: Tom Miller

COUNCILMEN

Oswald G. Wolf, Mayor Pro Tem
C. F. Alford
C. M. Bartholomew
Simon Gillis

May 1937 - May 1939

Mayor: Tom Miller

COUNCILMEN

Oswald G. Wolf, Mayor Pro Tem
C. F. Alford
C. M. Bartholomew
Simon Gillis

May 1939 - May 1941

Mayor: Tom Miller

COUNCILMEN

Oswald G. Wolf, Mayor Pro Tem
C. F. Alford
C. M. Bartholomew (Died September 1940. Council ap-
     pointed his son, E. C. Bartholomew, to the position)
Simon Gillis

138

May 1941 - May 1943

Mayor: Tom Miller

COUNCILMEN

Oswald G. Wolf, Mayor Pro Tem
C. F. Alford
E. C. Bartholomew
Simon Gillis

May 1943 - May 1945

Mayor: Tom Miller

COUNCILMEN

E. C. Bartholomew, Mayor Pro Tem
C. F. Alford
Simon Gillis
Oswald G. Wolf

May 1945 - May 1947

Mayor: Tom Miller

COUNCILMEN

E. C. Bartholomew, Mayor Pro Tem
Simon Gillis (resigned April 4, 1946)
Homer Thornberry (replaced Gillis on June 6, 1946)
C. F. Alford (died August 4, 1946)
Taylor Glass (elected September 9, 1946 to replace Alford)
Oswald G. Wolf

May 1947 - May 1949

Mayor: Tom Miller

139

COUNCILMEN

Homer Thornberry, Mayor Pro Tem (resigned May 27, 1948 to run for a congressional seat)
Taylor Glass (Glass became Mayor Pro Tem when Thornberry resigned)
E. C. Bartholomew
Will Johnson
Mrs. Stuart (Emma) Long (replaced Thornberry in October 1948)

May 1949 - May 1951

Mayor: Taylor Glass

COUNCILMEN

W. S. Drake, Mayor Pro Tem
Will T. Johnson
Emma Long
Stuart A. MacCorkle

May 1951 - May 1953

Mayor: W. S. Drake

COUNCILMEN

Stuart A. MacCorkle, Mayor Pro Tem
Will T. Johnson
Ben White
Emma Long

May 1953 - May 1955

Mayor: Charles McAden

COUNCILMEN

Wesley Pearson, Mayor Pro Tem
140

Ted Thompson
Emma Long
Ben White

May 1955 - May 1959

Mayor: Tom Miller

COUNCILMEN

Wesley Pearson, Mayor Pro Tem
Emma Long
Lester Palmer
Ben White

May 1959 - May 1961

Mayor: Tom Miller

COUNCILMEN

Lester Palmer, Mayor Pro Tem
Ben White
Hub Bechtol
Edgar H. Perry III

May 1961 - May 1963

Mayor: Lester Palmer

COUNCILMEN

Edgar H. Perry III, Mayor Pro Tem
Ben White
Bob Armstrong
Louis Shanks

May 1963 - May 1965

Mayor: Lester Palmer

COUNCILMEN

Travis LaRue, Mayor Pro Tem
Ben White
Emma Long
Louis Shanks

May 1965 - May 1967

Mayor: Lester Palmer

COUNCILMEN

Louis Shanks, Mayor Pro Tem
Ben White
Emma Long
Travis LaRue

May 1967 - May 1969

Mayor: Harry Akin

COUNCILMEN

Emma Long, Mayor Pro Tem
Dick Nichols
Ralph Janes
Travis LaRue

May 1969 - May 1971

Mayor: Travis LaRue

COUNCILMEN

The position of Mayor Pro Tem was alternated each four months among councilmen beginning with Stuart A. MacCorkle.

142

D. R. Price
Jay Johnson
Ralph Janes
Stuart A. MacCorkle
Joe Atkison
Les Gage

May 1971 - May 1973

Mayor: Roy Butler

COUNCILMEN

Dan Love, Mayor Pro Tem
Dr. Bud Dryden
Jeffrey Friedman
Lowell Lebermann
Dick Nichols
Berl Handcox

Appendix B

City Managers of the City of Austin

Adam R. Johnson	July 28, 1926 - June 1, 1933
Guiton Morgan	June 1, 1933 - September 19, 1940
James A. Garrison*	September 19, 1940 - March 16, 1941
Guiton Morgan	March 16, 1941 - April 14, 1942
Walter E. Seaholm*	April 14, 1942 - August 9, 1945
Guiton Morgan	August 9, 1945 - June 1, 1950
Walter E. Seaholm	June 1, 1950 - February 9, 1955
W. T. Williams, Jr.	February 9, 1955 - June 28, 1967
James A. Wilson*	June 28, 1967 - August 17, 1967
Reuben Rountree, Jr.*	August 17, 1967 - September 1, 1967
R. A. Tinstman	September 1, 1967 - August 28, 1969
Norman Barker*	August 28, 1969 - November 15, 1969
Lynn H. Andrews	November 15, 1969 - June 2, 1972
Dan H. Davidson*	May 4, 1972 - August 31, 1972
Dan H. Davidson	August 31, 1972 -

* Acting

Bibliography

American Statesman. September 16, 1880.

American Statesman. December 16, 1895.

Austin American. August 26, 1971.

Austin American. September 1, 1972.

Austin American-Statesman. April 6, 1909.

Austin City Council. *Minute Book A.* November 16, 1872.

Austin City Council. *Minute Book A.* February 13, 1871.

Austin City Council. *Minute Book E.* November 13, 1882.

Austin City Council. *Minute Book H.* June 1, 1892.

Austin Daily Statesman. April 20, 1909.

Austin Statesman. December 16, 1895.

Barkley, Mary Star. *History of Austin and Travis County 1839-1899.* Austin: Steck Company, 1963.

Charter of the City of Austin. Article II, Section 2, 1953.

Garland, C. H. *Public Management.* February, 1932.

The International City Management Association. *Council Manager Plan.* Chicago, 1966.

Johnson, Adam R. *A Brief History of Austin's City Government Since the Inauguration of Council-Manager Form of Government.* Austin, 1932.

MacCorkle, Stuart A. *American Municipal Government and Administration.* Boston, 1948.

———. "A Professor Becomes a Councilman." *Texas Municipalities.* Vol. XXXVII, No. 8, pp. 201-205.

———. "Two Years at City Hall." *Austin American-Statesman.* April 25, 1971.

———. "Who Really Fathered the City-Manager Plan?" *One American City.* March, 1966, pp. 106-107.

Overbeck, Ruth Ann. *Alexander Penn Wooldridge.* Austin, 1963.

Robertson, J. W., ed. *Charter and Revised Ordinances of the City of Austin.* Charter Article 4. Austin: Texas Capitol Book and Job Office, 1878.

Ruggles, Gardner and Johnson, I. D. *Charter and Revised Civil Ordinances.* Charter Article VIII.

San Antonio Light and Gazette. March 30, 1910.

Standing Committees of the City Council for the Term Ending April 1909. Austin-Travis County Collection.

Stone, Harold; Price, Don K.; Stone, Kathryn H. *City Manager Government in Austin* (Texas). Chicago, 1939.

Texas, Congress, House. An *Act to Incorporate the City of Austin, to Grant It a New Charter and to Extend Its Boundaries.* H.B. 636, Sections 3, 16, 34.

Texas, House Bill 636, Sections 4 and 5.

Western City. Vol. XV, No. 1. January, 1939.

Index

150

153

154